D0309237

AN ILLUSTRATED GUIDE TO
ALLIED
FIGHTERS
OF WORLD WAR II

AN ILLUSTRATED GUIDE TO
ALLIED
FIGHTERS
OF WORLD WAR II

Bill Gunston

a Salamander book

Published by Salamander Books Limited
LONDON

A Salamander Book

© 1981 Salamander Books Ltd.,
Salamander House,
27 Old Gloucester Street,
London WC1N 3AF,
United Kingdom

ISBN 0 86101 081 7

Distributed in the United Kingdom by
New English Library Ltd.

All rights reserved. No part of this
book may be reproduced, stored in a
retrieval system or transmitted in any
form or by any means, electronic,
mechanical, photocopying, recording
or otherwise, without the prior
permission of Salamander Books Ltd.

Contents

Aircraft are arranged alphabetically by manufacturers' names, within
national groups

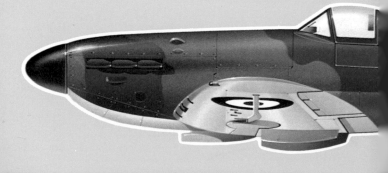

Credits

Author: Bill Gunston, former Technical Editor of *Flight International*, Assistant Compiler of *Jane's All the World's Aircraft*, contributor to many Salamander illustrated reference books.

Editor: Ray Bonds
Designer: Lloyd Martin

Colour and line drawings: © Pilot Press Ltd.
Photographs: The publishers wish to thank all the official international governmental archives, aircraft and systems manufacturers and private collections who have supplied photographs for this book.

Printed in Belgium by Henri Proost et Cie.

FRANCE

During the 1930s French aircraft companies flew some 150 different types of military aircraft. Many were notorious for their ugliness, but from 1935 the Gallic designers created increasingly competitive designs which could have been the basis for airpower that not even Hitler could have scorned.

Sadly, the morale of France was poor. In 1936 a newly elected Left-Wing government nationalised all defence industries, ripping all the old companies apart and forming giant conglomerate groups on a purely geographical basis. Far from increasing output, it caused chaos; and the excellent designs that remained with the tattered surviving private firms were denied essential parts and suffered delay of a year or more. Even the nationalised projects were surrounded by malcontents and saboteurs who crippled production despite increasingly desperate efforts by the dedicated majority.

Another important factor was that available engines were hardly powerful enough to make French fighters adequate when the stern test came. Lorraine and Farman virtually gave up. Hispano-Suiza had a basically good vee-12 which by 1935 was type-tested at 860hp and in World War II was to be the basis for over 100,000 engines made in the Soviet Union at up to 1,650hp. But the only fighter available to the Armée de l'Air in really large numbers in 1939, the M.S. 406, was stuck with 860hp, so that when it met the Bf 109E it was shot down in droves.

The 48th Dewoitine D 520 off the SNCA du Midi production line, destined for service with GC I/3 at sunny Cannes-Mandelieu. The D 520 was the best of the French fighters available in quantity.

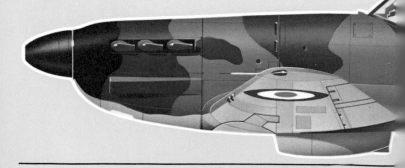

Gnome-Rhône, from 1921 a licensee of Bristol, purchased a licence for the British company's 1,375hp Hercules sleeve-valve radial, but never got into wartime production. Instead all it could offer in production was a radial that was hard-pressed to give 1,000hp, and this was fitted to the basically formidable Bloch 151 series. The power was simply not enough, and one of the enduring memories of the Bloch was of the number that managed to limp back shot to ribbons but unbowed. Ability to take punishment is desirable in a fighter, but not the way to win.

Apart from the splendid prototypes by engineers Vernisse and Galtier at the Arsenal de l'Aéronautique, which did not reach the squadrons, the best homegrown fighter of World War II is judged to have been the Dewoitine 520. This had the Hispano vee-12 at 910hp, and was small, light and agile enough to do well. If only the workers had "pulled their finger out" a year earlier the Luftwaffe's 109s would not have had quite such an easy time over France.

As it was, the frantic French government had by 1938 turned elsewhere for fighters and placed massive orders in the USA. One type, the Curtiss Hawk 75, reached the squadrons in significant numbers and even managed to achieve near-parity with the 109 despite a poorer flight performance. By the time the other US types were in their crates, France had fallen.

DEWOITINE D.520 N°48

Bloch MB-152C-1
MB-150 to 157 (data for 152)

Origin: SNCASO.

Type: Single-seat fighter.

Engine: 1,080hp Gnome-Rhône 14N-25 14-cylinder radial.

Dimensions: Span 34ft 6¾in (10·5m); length 29ft 10in (9·1m); height 13ft 0in (3·95m).

Weights: Empty 4,453lb (2020kg); loaded 5,842lb (2650kg).

Performance: Maximum speed 323mph (520km/h); climb to 16,400ft (5000m) in 6 minutes; service ceiling 32,800ft (10,000m); range 373 miles (600km).

Armament: Two 20mm Hispano 404 cannon (60-round drum) and two 7·5mm MAC 1934 machine guns (500 rounds each); alternatively four MAC 1934.

History: First flight (MB-150) October 1937; (MB-151) 18 August 1938; (MB-152) December 1938; (MB-155) 3 December 1939; (MB-157) March 1942.

Users: France (Armée de l'Air, Vichy AF), Greece, Romania.

Development: Like so many French aircraft of the time, the Bloch monoplane fighter story began badly, got into its stride just in time for the capitulation and eventually produced outstanding aircraft which were unable to be used. The prototype 150 was not only ugly but actually failed to fly, the frightened test pilot giving up on 17 July 1936. It was only after redesign with more power and larger wing that the aircraft finally left the ground. Bloch had been absorbed into the new nationalised industry as part of SNCASO and five of the new group's factories were put to work making 25. But the detail design was difficult to make, so the MB-151 was produced with the hope that 180 would be made each month from late 1938. Orders

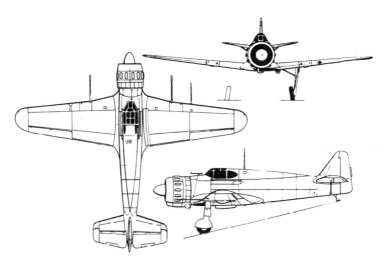

Above: MB-152; note the canted engine to reduce engine torque.

were also placed for the slightly more powerful MB-152, but by the start of World War II only 85 Blochs had been delivered and not one was fit for use; all lacked gunsights and most lacked propellers! Eventually, after overcoming desperate problems and shortages, 593 were delivered by the capitulation, equipping GC I/1, II/1, I/8, II/8, II/9, II/10, III/10 and III/0. The Germans impressed 173 surviving Bloch 151 and 152 fighters, passing 20 to Romania. The MB-155 had a 1,180hp engine and was used by Vichy France. The ultimate model was the superb MB-157, with 1,580hp 14R-4 engine and 441mph (710km/h) speed, never put into production. By this time the firm's founder had changed his name to Dassault.

Left: 152-C1 (C1 = chasse, 1 seat) flying with GC II/1 (GC = Groupe de Chasse) in May 1940. Bloch delivered 140 MB-151 and 488 MB-152, the serial numbers on the tail running unbroken.

Below left: A line-up of 152s; by the French collapse Bloch fighters had gained 188 air-combat victories for the loss of 86 pilots killed, wounded or missing.

Below: First production example of the longer-ranged MB-155, flown in April 1940.

Dewoitine D 520

D 520S

Origin: SNCA du Midi.
Type: Single-seat fighter.
Engine: One 910hp Hispano-Suiza 12Y-45 vee-12 liquid-cooled.
Dimensions: Span 33ft 5¾in (10·2m); length 28ft 8½in (8·75m); height 11ft 3in (3·4m).
Weights: Empty 4,630lb (2100kg); loaded 6,173lb (2800kg).
Performance: Maximum speed 329mph (530km/h); initial climb 2,362ft (720m)/min; service ceiling 36,090ft (11,000m); range 777 miles (1240km).
Armament: One 20mm Hispano-Suiza 404 cannon, with 60 rounds, firing through the propeller hub, and four 7·5mm MAC 1934 machine guns, each with 500 rounds, in wings.
History: First flight (520–01) 2 October 1938; (production, 520-2) 3 December 1939; service delivery 1 February 1940.
Users: Bulgaria, France, Italy (RA), Romania.

Development: Few people have ever disputed that this neat little fighter was the best produced in France prior to the Armistice; it was certainly the best to reach the squadrons. Unlike so many other hopeful types which just failed to be ready in time, the D 520 made it — but only just. The great Marcel Doret did not help when, having made a splendid first test flight, he forgot

Above: The D 520 was adopted by the collaborative Vichy government as its standard fighter, and saw service against the Allies, as well as with Axis air forces. This example was No 147, delivered prior to France's capitulation in 1940.

Right: Production of the D 520 resumed in 1941 when, under German control, the SNCA du Midi was merged into SNCASE, and manufacture picked up again at Toulouse-Blagnac. This example is fresh off the line.

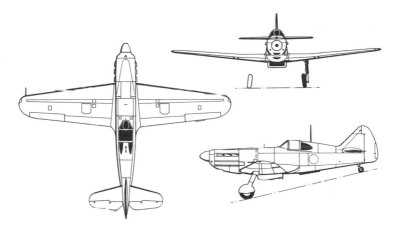

Above: Standard D 520 with folded ventral radio mast.

about the retractable landing gear on 27 November 1938 and put the first prototype out of action. The new fighter was a direct development of the 500 series and though it was very small it was hoped to fit an engine of 1,300hp — but nothing suitable was available. The first prototype had an open cockpit and the second still had a curved windscreen, tailskid and two drum-fed machine guns, as did the first production machine. But the second was up to production standard. The Dewoitine plants had vanished into the nationalised SNCA du Midi under the law of 1936 and these were meant to deliver ten in September 1939 and 30 in October. Actually timing ran about three months late, but with the panic in 1940 industry went mad. In May 1940 101 were delivered and by June the output had reached ten per day, a figure seldom exceeded by any aircraft plant in history. GC I/3 was first to go into action, followed in late May by GC II/3, with III/3, III/6 and II/7 following before the capitulation. These groups were credited with 147 kills for the loss of 85 fighters and 44 pilots. Subsequently the Vichy government restored the D 520 to production, 740 being built in all. In 1942 the Luftwaffe seized 411, passing many to Italy, Romania and Bulgaria. But in 1944 GC I/8 was re-formed under Doret and, after painting out the German insignia, went into action against the last German pockets in southern France.

Morane-Saulnier M.S.406

M.S.405, M.S.406C-1

Origin: Aeroplanes Morane-Saulnier; also assembled by SNCAO at St Nazaire-Bouguenais; variant built under licence by Dornier-Werke, Switzerland.

Type: Single-seat fighter.

Engine: One 860hp Hispano-Suiza 12Y-31 vee-12 liquid-cooled.

Dimensions: Span 34ft 9¾in (10·60m); length 26ft 9¼in (8·16m); height 9ft 3¾in (2·83m).

Weights: (406) empty 4,189lb (1900kg); loaded 5,364–5,445lb; maximum loaded 6,000lb (2722kg).

Performance: Maximum speed 302mph (485km/h); initial climb 2,789ft (850m)/min; service ceiling 30,840ft (9400m); range (without external tanks) 497 miles (800km).

Armament: One 20mm Hispano-Suiza HS-9 or 404 cannon with drum of 60 rounds, and two 7·5mm MAC 1934 in wings each with 300 rounds.

History: First flight (405) 8 August 1935; (production 405) 3 February 1938; (production 406) 29 January 1939; service delivery (406) 1 March 1939.

Users: Croatia, Finland, France, Germany, Turkey; ordered by China, Lithuania and Poland but for various reasons never in service with these countries.

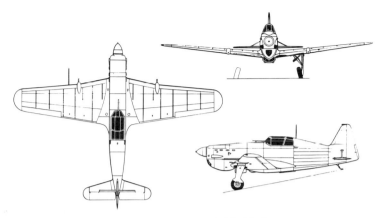

Above: M.S.406-C1, with ventral aerial folded.

Development: After their unbroken series of parasol monoplanes Morane-Saulnier built the M.S.405 secretly to meet a 1934 specification of the Armée de l'Air. Compared with other fighters at the start of World War II it was underpowered, lacking in performance and somewhat lacking in firepower. On the other hand its early start meant it was at least available, while other French fighters were mainly a vast collection of prototypes. ▶

Left: The 704th production M.S.406-C1, serving in early 1940 with 1e Escadrille, GC I/2 at Nîmes. The radiator between the landing gears could be wound in or out (in the picture below it is fully extended) and the ventral radio aerial was extended vertically down, in the air.

Below: One of the first operational units to be equipped with the M.S.406 was GC I/7, which began conversion in 1938. They went to North Africa in 1939, and this 1940 photograph shows them in the Lebanon.

Above: Fodder for 109s, a Battle of the Advanced Air Striking Force visits a Groupe de Chasse equipped with Moranes in 1940.

Altogether 17 M.S.405 were built, most becoming prototypes of proposed future versions and ultimately giving rise to the Swiss D-3800 series of fighters which, unlike most 405s, did not have a retractable radiator. An unusual feature was the fact that, except for the fabric-covered rear fuselage, most of the covering was Plymax (light alloy bonded to plywood). The M.S.406 was the 405 production version incorporating all the requested modifications. The production was shared out among the nationalised groups (Morane retaining only a small part of the work), with production lines at Bouguenais and Puteaux. By the time of the collapse in June 1940 no fewer than 1,081 had been completed, despite a desperate shortage of engines. In May 1940 the 406 equipped 19 of the 26 French combat-ready fighter groups. One who flew them said they were "free from vices, but too slow to catch German aircraft and too badly armed to shoot them down. Poorly protected, our own losses were high". The Vichy government fitted 32gal drop tanks to Moranes sent to Syria to fight the RAF. Many were used by Finland, fitted with skis and often with Soviet M-105P engines of higher power (the so-called LaGG-Morane).

Below: Moranes of a Free Polish unit (aircraft No 1031 is nearest the camera). Previously Moranes had been shipped to Poland.

Above: This 406-C1 shows the radiator fully extended, sloping main wheels and crude ring-and-bead auxiliary gunsight.

Potez 63 series

630, 631, 633, 637 and 63·11

Origin: Avions Henri Potez.
Type: (630, 631) two- (sometimes three-) seat day and night fighter; (633) two-seat light attack bomber; (63.11) three-seat army co-operation and reconnaissance.
Engines: (630) two 725hp Hispano-Suiza 14AB 14-cylinder two-row radials; all other versions, two 700hp Gnome-Rhône 14M of same layout.
Dimensions: Span 52ft 6in (16m); length 36ft 4in (11·07m); (63·11 only) 36ft 1in; (11m); height 11ft 9¾in (3·6m).
Weights: Empty (630, 631, 633) typically 5,730lb (2600kg); (637) 6,390lb (2900kg); (63·11) 6,912lb (3205kg); maximum loaded (631) 8,235lb (3735kg); (633, 637) 9,285lb (4210kg); (63·11) 9,987lb (4530kg).
Performance: Maximum speed (630, 631, 633) 273mph (440km/h); (637) 267mph (430km/h); (63·11) 264mph (425km/h); initial climb (typical) 1,800ft (550m)/min; service ceiling (630, 631) 32,800ft (10,000m); (others, typical) 26,250ft (8000m).
Armament: See "Development" text.
History: First flight (Potez 63) 25 April 1936; (production 630) February 1938; (prototype 63·11) December 1938.
Users: France, Germany (Luftwaffe), Greece, Romania, Switzerland.

Development: Winner of a 1934 competition for a C3 (three-seat fighter) for the Armée de l'Air, the Potez 63 was a clean twin-finned machine powered by two of the new Hispano slim radials. It soon branched into a host of sub-variants, including many for foreign customers. The first 80 production aircraft were 630s, but they were soon grounded due to severe engine failure after only a few hours. The 631, however, was more successful and 208 were delivered (121 in May 1940 alone), equipping five fighter squadrons, two Aéronavale squadrons and many other units and shooting down 29 German aircraft (12 by the navy squadrons) in the Battle for France. Most had two (some only one) 20mm Hispano 9 or 404 cannon, one or two 7·5mm MAC in the rear cockpit and, from February 1940, six MAC faired under the outer wings. The 633 had only two machine guns, one forward-firing and the other in the rear cockpit, and the profusion of export variants had several different kinds of gun. Maximum bomb load was 1,323lb (600kg), including 880lb (400kg) internal. Many 633s had a busy war, Greek examples fighting with the Allies and Romanian examples fighting the Russians. The 637 was used in numbers in May 1940 but was only a stop-gap for the 63·11, with glazed nose and humped rear canopy, which was used in large numbers by the Luftwaffe, Vichy French, Free French and others. Over 900 were built, bringing the total for the 63 family to more than 1,300.

Below: Mass-produced three-seat reconnaissance Potez 63.II, No 831, which joined the Allies in North Africa.

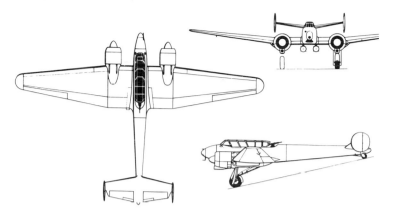

Above: The Potez 633 bomber, used mainly by export customers.

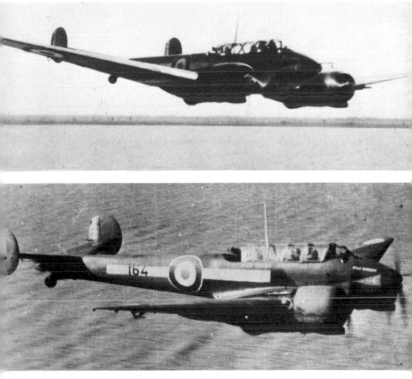

Above: Two photographs of a Potez 631 twin-engined fighter of 4ᵉ Escadrille, GCN II/3, one of the world's first dedicated night-fighter units since 1918. Note the six machine guns under the outer wings, just visible in the upper view. After the Armistice all Vichy aircraft were painted with prominent red/yellow stripes over their engines and tail units, ostensibly to indicate neutrality.

GREAT BRITAIN

Apart from Italy, Britain was the only country to see the famed Schneider Trophy races through to the bitter end. The final winner was Reginald Mitchell's Supermarine S.6B seaplane. It is often held that this led to his Spitfire, but similarities are almost non-existent. Far more important was the fact that the thrashing of its special engine greatly assisted Rolls-Royce to develop the PV.12 from which stemmed the Merlin, and though this was small by comparison it had just enough power to keep abreast of the big Daimler-Benz in the Bf 109. (One thing it lacked was direct fuel injection, which allowed the German pilots to do negative-g manoeuvres without the engine cutting out.)

One cannot over-emphasize the importance of the Merlin, which in the Hurricane won the Battle of Britain. The Spitfire, one of the first British aircraft to adopt modern stressed-skin construction, came later. The Hurricane was strong and easy to repair, but had to be flown with great dash and skill to beat a 109, whereas the Spit could outfly the enemy in almost all respects but would have benefited from a shell-firing cannon or long-range gun earlier in the war. Later it was to be discovered that, possibly by chance, its odd elliptical wing had a cross-section which enabled it to dive faster than any other aircraft, to at least Mach 0.92. In fact, during the 1950s it was realised that it was a much better wing than the later ''laminar-flow'' wing that

One major fault of pre-war RAF procurement was belief in the fighter armed only with a turret. This example is a Defiant I as flown by the CO of the first squadron, No 264.

replaced it on the Spiteful and jet Attacker.

High-Mach performance was of limited relevance to fighting the Luftwaffe, however, and the chief importance of the Spitfire was its incredible ability to develop with more power, more fuel, more cannon, more bombs, naval equipment and everything else which, if it did not include the kitchen sink, did include full-size beer barrels flown on the belly racks to troops in the Normandy beachhead! The "Spit" was more important than all other British fighters combined, and it might have helped the Allied cause if all other British fighters had been cancelled except the long-range radar-equipped Mosquito.

Sydney Camm's Typhoon was a disappointment as a fighter, but very useful for catching hit-and-run raiders at low level and bagging them in a straight chase. Later it was even more valuable as a ground-attack aircraft with bombs and rockets. The Tempest, with a better airframe, was the top killer of flying boats, and the Mosquito was a superb night fighter that did more than any other aircraft to sap the morale of the Luftwaffe by night. In 1940 the Beaufighter — like the Mosquito the product of persistence by designers, not any order by the RAF — at last combined radar with good performance and devastating firepower, while in July 1944 the first batch of 16 Meteor Is joined a flight of 616 Sqn, the first regular turbojet unit in the world.

Blackburn Skua and Roc

Skua II, Roc I

Origin: The Blackburn Aircraft Company, Brough; Roc production assigned to Boulton Paul Aircraft, Wolverhampton.
Type: (S) two-seat carrier fighter/dive bomber; (R) two-seat carrier fighter.
Engine: 905hp Bristol Perseus XII nine-cylinder sleeve-valve radial.
Dimensions: Span (S) 46ft 2in (14·07m), (R) 46ft 0in (14·02m); length (S) 35ft 7in (10·85m), (R) 35ft 0in (10·67m); height 12ft 5in (3·79m).
Weights: Empty (S) 5,490lb (2490kg), (R) 6,121lb (2776kg); maximum (S) 8,228lb (3732kg), (R) 8,800lb (3992kg).
Performance: Maximum speed (S) 225mph (362km/h), (R) 196mph (315km/h); service ceiling 20,200ft (6157m); range (typical) 800 miles (1287km).
Armament: (S) four 0·303in Browning fixed in wings, one 0·303in Lewis or Vickers K in rear cockpit, 500lb (227kg) bomb on hinged arms under fuselage, light bombs under wings; (R) four 0·303in Browning in power dorsal turret, light bombs under wings.
History: First flight (S) 9 February 1937, (R) 23 December 1938; service delivery (S) November 1938, (R) April 1939.
User: UK (RN).

Development: The Skua was designed to a 1934 specification, O.27/34, for a naval dive bomber. Two prototypes powered by 840hp Mercury engines looked sleek against the Navy's fabric-covered biplanes, and eventually 190 were built to a later requirement (25/36), to enter service as the Fleet Air Arm's first monoplane and first with v-p propeller or retractable landing gear. During the first year of war the Skuas worked hard, and made many gallant attacks on German capital ships. On 26 September 1939

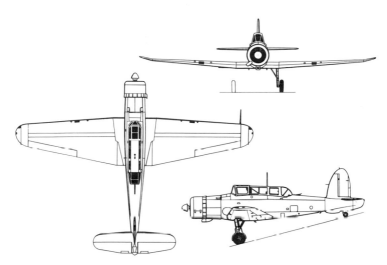

Above: Blackburn Skua II, the dive-bomber version.

Skuas of 803 Sqn from *Ark Royal* shot down a Do 18, the first Luftwaffe aircraft destroyed by Britain. But the basic aircraft was underpowered, and by 1941 the Skua was becoming a target tug and trainer. Likewise the 136 turreted Rocs were even less capable of surviving, let alone acting as fighters. The 136 built, to O.30/35, never served on a carrier and were soon withdrawn. A few were seaplanes, with Shark-type floats.

Below: A fine study of the 28th Roc, which despite retaining its turret was used as a testbed for the sleeve-valve engine.

Boulton Paul P.82 Defiant
Defiant I and II (data for I)

Origin: Boulton Paul Aircraft, Wolverhampton.
Type: Two-seat fighter.
Engine: I, 1,030hp Rolls-Royce Merlin III vee-12 liquid-cooled; II, 1,260hp Merlin 20.
Dimensions: Span 39ft 4in (12m); length 35ft 4in (10·75m); height 12ft 2in (3·7m).
Weights: Empty 6,000lb (2722kg); loaded 8,350lb (3787kg).
Performance: Maximum speed 303mph (488km/h); initial climb 1,900ft (579m)/min; service ceiling 30,500ft (9300m); range, probably about 500 miles (805km).
Armament: Hydraulically operated dorsal gun turret with four 0·303in Browning machine guns, each with 600 rounds.
History: First flight (prototype) 11 August 1937; (production Mk I) 30 July 1939; first delivery December 1939.
User: UK (RAF).

Development: By 1933 military staffs were intensely studying the en-closed gun turret, manually worked or power-driven, either to defend a bomber or to arm a fighter. A primitive form was seen on the Hawker Demon in 1936, while in France the *Multiplace de Combat* class of aircraft were huge fighters with turrets all over. The Defiant was a bold attempt to combine the performance of the new monoplanes with a powered enclosed turret carrying four 0·303in Brownings, each with 600 rounds. The gunner, behind the pilot, had a control column moved left/right for rotation, fore/aft for depression and elevation and with a safety/firing button on top. The Defiant itself was a clean and pleasant aircraft, but rather degraded in per-formance by carrying a crew of two and the heavy turret. No 264 Sqn went into action on 12 May 1940 in desperate fights over the Low Countries. On the 13th six escorted Battle bombers, and only one returned; it seemed the ▶

Right: As it carried a second crew-member the Defiant was judged a good basis for a dedicated night fighter, with airborne-interception radar. From the start of the "night Blitz" many Defiants, particularly those of 141 and 264 Sqns, operated by night but without radar. In 1941 no fewer than seven squadrons received Defiants with radar, including this Mk IA with AI.V.

Below: Without radar but a later aircraft, AA436 was a Defiant II serving with one of the world's first (1917 with Sopwith Camels) night-fighter squadrons, No 151. Note the two ventral radio aerial masts which were retracted prior to landing.

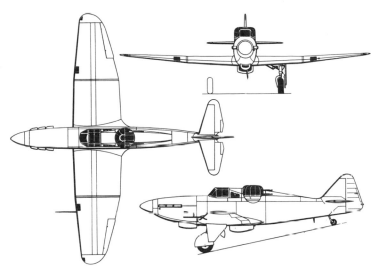

Above: Defiant I with turret fairings raised and masts folded.

Defiant was a failure against the Bf 109E. But seven days later remnants of 264 shot down "17 Messerschmitts without loss" and later on the same day destroyed eleven Ju 87s and 88s. Once the enemy were familiar with the Defiant it had had its day by daylight, but it did well in 1940—41 as a night fighter and was later fitted with radar. Most of the 1,064 built served as night fighters, target tugs and in air/sea rescue in Britain, the Middle East and Far East. Defiants carried the Mandrel jamming system to confuse German defences.

Right: This black-painted Defiant II was the subject for the profile drawing at the foot of the preceding pages. In this late-1942 photograph the rear radio mast is retracted and the rear turret fairing is in the lowered combat-ready position. For full turret usage round 360° the pilot had to shut his hood and the gunner then retracted the forward fairing as well. The oil cooler and radiator of the Mk II were both deeper than on the Mk I aircraft, but manoeuvrability remained poor.

Below: In its heyday: 264 Sqn in March 1940, just ready for ops.

Bristol Type 156 Beaufighter
Beaufighter I to TF.X (data mainly Mk X)

Origin: Bristol Aeroplane Company, Filton and Weston-Super-Mare; also Department of Aircraft Production, Australia.

Type: Two-seat torpedo strike fighter (other marks, night fighters, target tugs).

Engines: Two 1,770hp Bristol Hercules XVII 14-cylinder sleeve-valve radials; (Mk II) 1,250hp R-R Merlin XX; (other marks) different Hercules; (one-offs had R-R Griffons and Wright GR-2600 Cyclones).

Dimensions: Span 57ft 10in (17·63m); length 41ft 8in (12·6m) (II, 42ft 9in); height 15ft 10in (4·84m).

Weights: Empty 15,600lb (7100kg) (I, II, 13,800lb; VI, XI, 14,900lb); loaded 25,400lb (11,530kg) (most other marks 21,000lb, 9525kg).

Performance: Maximum speed 312mph (502km/h) (fighter marks, 330mph, 528km/h); initial climb 1,850ft (564m)/min; service ceiling 26,500ft (8077m) (fighters, 30,000ft, 9144m); range 1,540 miles (2478km).

Armament: Four 20mm Hispano cannon fixed in underside of forward fuselage (initially hand loaded with 60-round drums, later with belt feed), and one 0·303in Vickers K aimed by observer (fighters, also six 0·303in Brownings, two fixed in outer left wing and four in right. One 1,605lb (728kg) torpedo on centreline or 2,127lb (954kg) and wing racks for eight rocket projectiles or two 1,000lb (454kg) bombs.

History: First flight (Type 156 prototype) 17 July 1939; (production Mk I) May 1940; service delivery 27 July 1940; first flight (Mk 21, Australia) 26 May 1944; last delivery from new (UK) September 1945, (Australia) October 1945.

Users: Australia, Canada; New Zealand, South Africa, UK (RAF), US (AAF); other countries post-war.

Development: During the critical years 1935—39 the most glaring gap in the RAF's armoury was the lack of any long-range fighter, any cannon-armed fighter and any fighter capable of effective bomber escort and night fighting. Leslie Frise and engine designer Fedden talked at length of the possibility of creating a single type out of the Blenheim and Beaufort

Right: R2059 was the seventh production aircraft, delivered (minus the AI Mk IV radar, fitted later) in August 1940. It served with 25 Sqn at North Weald, north-east of London. Aircraft of these early batches lacked the wing machine guns, which again were fitted later. The first 400 also had cannon which had to be laboriously reloaded with 60-round drums by the observer.

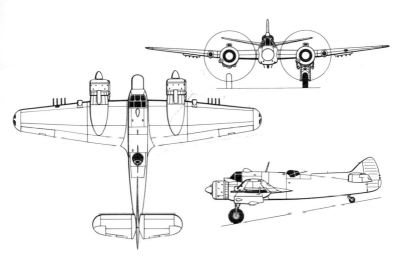

Above: Beaufighter TF.X with rear gun, radar and rocket rails.

families that could meet all demands, but no official requirement was forth-
coming — other than the strange F.11/37 Specification for a fighter with a
heavily armed cannon turret. Eventually the two Bristol leaders did the
obvious thing: they proposed a new twin-Hercules two-seater carrying
enough armament to blast anything in front of it out of the sky. By using the
wing, tail, landing gear, systems and jigs of the Beaufort it could be put into
production quickly. The Air Ministry was enthusiastic and the first of what
was to be an historic war-winning aeroplane took the air only six months
later. A snub-nosed battleship, it was immensely strong, surprisingly
manoeuvrable and a great basis for development. Almost its only operational
shortcoming was a tendency to swing on takeoff or landing, and instability
at low speeds, which later addition of a large dorsal fin and dihedral tailplane
did not fully cure.

Early models barely exceeded 300mph with low-power Hercules and, in
the absence of Griffon engines, 450 were fitted with Merlins, but these were ▶

Left: A much later "Beau", this was one
of the first batch of Coastal TF.X built
at Weston. Serving with 455 Sqn, it is
shown with rear defence gun (a belt-fed
Browning in this mark) and underwing
rockets. Later the Mk X supplemented the
dihedralled tailplane with a large dorsal
fin to improve asymmetric handling and
reduce swing on takeoff and landing. All
TF (torpedo/fighter) aircraft had provision
for either the British 18-inch or US
22.5-inch torpedo.

Above: A fine picture of a Mk VIC of RAF No 455 Sqn firing its underwing rockets — probably just for the benefit of the photographer, since the aircraft is flying straight and level.

less powerful and accentuated instability. Speed was soon judged less important when the need for night fighters to beat the Blitz became urgent. Equipped with AI Mk IV radar the early deliveries to 25 and 29 Sqns were a major reason for the Luftwaffe giving up the Blitz on Britain. Eventually the "Beau" served on all fronts, having thimble-nose AI Mk VII in 1942, torpedoes in 1943, rockets in 1944 and a spate of special installations in 1945. A total of 5,564 were built in England and 364 in Australia, the last fighter and torpedo versions serving with Coastal Command, the Far East Air Force and the RAAF until 1960. To the Luftwaffe it was a feared opponent even 500 miles out in the Atlantic; to the Japanese it was "Whispering death" so named because of the quietness of the sleeve-valve engines. It was sheer luck the "Beau" could be produced in time.

Left: Probably taken in Tunisia in early 1943, this photograph shows a war-weary Mk VI, with structural provision for AI.VIII radar but nothing actually fitted except the forward-ident lamp.

Below: Red-doped fabric covers the muzzles of this Mk IF taxiing on Malta; it also has outer-wing bomb racks, but no radar

De Havilland 98 Mosquito

D.H.98 Mosquito I to 43

Origin: The de Havilland Aircraft Company, Hatfield and Leavesden; also built by Airspeed, Percival Aircraft and Standard Motors (Canley); de Havilland Aircraft Pty, Australia; de Havilland Aircraft of Canada.

Type: Designed as high-speed day bomber, see text for subsequent variants.

Engines: (Mks II, III, IV and early VI) two 1,230hp Rolls-Royce Merlin 21 or (late FB.VI) 1,635hp Merlin 25; (Mk IX) 1,680hp Merlin 72; (Mk XVI) Merlin 72 or 1,710hp Merlin 73 or 77; (Mk 30) 1,710hp Merlin 76; (Mk 33) 1,640hp Merlin 25; (Mks 34, 35, 36) 1,690hp Merlin 113/114. Many other variants had corresponding Merlins made by Packard.

Dimensions: Span (except Mk XV) 54ft 2in (16·5m); length (most common) 40ft 6in (12·34m); (bombers) 40ft 9½in; (radar-equipped fighters and Mks 34–38) typically 41ft 9in; (Mk 39) 43ft 4in; height (most common) 15ft 3½in (4·66m).

Weights: Empty (Mks II–VI) about 14,100lb; (Mks VIII–30) about 15,200lb; (beyond Mk 30) about 15,900–16,800lb; maximum gross (Mks II and III) around 17,500lb; (Mks IV and VI) about 22,500lb; (later night fighters) about 20,500lb (but HF.XV only 17,395lb); (Mks IX, XVI and marks beyond 30) typically 25,000lb (11,340kg).

Performance: Maximum speed, from 300mph (TT.39 with M4 sleeve) to 370mph (595km/h) for early night fighters, 380mph (612km/h) for III, IV and VI, 410mph (660km/h) for IX, XVI and 30, and 425mph for 34 and 35; service ceiling, from 30,000ft (9144m) for low-rated naval versions to 34,500ft (10,520m) for most marks, to around 40,000ft (12,190m) for high-blown versions, with Mk XV reaching 44,000ft (13,410m); combat range, typically 1,860 miles (2990km), with naval TFs down at 1,260 miles and PR.34 up to 3,500 miles.

Armament: See text.

History: See text.

Users: Australia, Belgium, Canada, China, Czechoslovakia, France, Jugoslavia, New Zealand, Norway, Soviet Union, Turkey, UK (RAF, RN, BOAC), US (AAF).

continued ▶

Right: Last and most formidable of all the wartime fighter marks, the NF.XXX (NF.30) had high-blown engines and paddle-blade propellers giving performance superior to anything in the Luftwaffe except the jets, at all heights up to over 35,000 feet.

Below: In contrast, the first fighter version was the F.II, seen here defending Malta with 23 Sqn in 1942. Most had AI.IV radar.

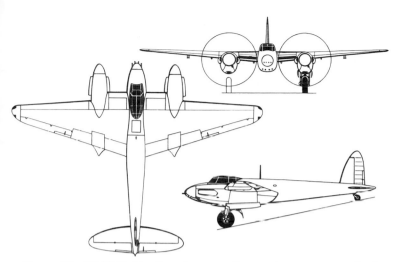

Above: The FB.VI fighter/bomber was the most numerous variant.

Development: The de Havilland Aircraft Co planned the Mosquito in October 1938 as a high-speed unarmed day bomber, with the added attraction of wooden construction to ease the strain on Britain's hard-pressed materials suppliers. The Air Ministry showed no interest, suggesting instead the Hatfield plant should make wings for existing heavy bombers. In 1940, with extreme reluctance, it was agreed to allow the firm to proceed, the only role thought possible for an unarmed aircraft being reconnaissance. The first prototype, built secretly at Salisbury Hall by a team which grew from 12 in January 1940 to 30 in the summer, was flown painted yellow on 25 November 1940. From it stemmed 7,781 aircraft, built in Britain, Canada and Australia, of the following types:

PR.I Unarmed photo-reconnaissance, with span lengthened from 52ft 6in of prototype to 54ft 2in but still with short engine nacelles.

F.II Night fighter, with pilot and observer side by side, flat bullet-proof windscreen, extended nacelles (as in all subsequent aircraft, with flaps divided into inner and outer segments) and armament of four 20mm Hispano cannon with 300 rounds each under the floor and four 0·303in Brownings with 2,000 rounds each in the nose. First flew 15 May 1941; subsequently fitted with AI Mk IV or V radar or Turbinlight searchlight.

T.III Dual-control trainer, first flown January 1942 but produced mainly after the war (last delivery 1949).

B.IV Unarmed bomber, carrying four 500lb (227kg) bombs internally; first delivered to 105 Sqn at Swanton Morley November 1941, making first operational sortie (Cologne, the morning after the first 1,000-bomber night attack) on 31 May 1942. Some later fitted with bulged bomb bays for 4,000lb (1814kg) bomb.

FB.VI Fighter-bomber and intruder, by day or night; same guns as F.II but two 250lb (113kg) bombs in rear bay and two more (later two 500lb) on wing racks; alternatively, 50 or 100 gal drop tanks, mines, depth charges or eight 60lb rockets. Some fitted with AI radar. Total production 2,584, more than any other mark.

B.VII Canadian-built Mk IV, used in North America only.

PR.VIII Reconnaissance conversion of B.IV with high-blown Merlin 61.

Mk IX Important advance in bomber (B.IX) and reconnaissance (PR.IX) versions; high-blown two-stage engines, bulged bomb bay for 4,000lb bomb or extra fuel, much increased weight, paddle-blade propellers and new avionics (Rebecca, Boozer, Oboe or H_2S Mk VI).

NF.XII Conversion of F.II fitted with new thimble nose containing AI Mk VIII centimetric radar in place of Brownings.

NF.XIII Similar to Mk XII but built as new, with thimble or bull nose and same wing as Mk VI for drop tanks or other stores; flew August 1943.

Above: A fine portrait of a Mosquito FB.VI. NT193 was a Hatfield-built example of this prolific mark, though many others were built by shadow factories and in Canada and Australia, with minor differences. The universal wing was plumbed for drop tanks but is seen here fitted with pylons for stores such as 500 lb (227 kg) bombs. Radar was not fitted.

NF.XV High-altitude fighter with wings extended to 59ft, pressurised cockpit, lightened structure, AI Mk VIII in nose and belly pack of four 0·303in Brownings to combat Ju 86P raiders.

Mk XVI Further major advance with two-stage Merlins, bulged bomb bay and pressurised cockpit. PR.XVI flew July 1943; B.XVI in January 1944, over 1,200 of latter being used for high-level nuisance raids with 4,000lb bombs.

NF.XVII Night fighter with new AI Mk X or SCR.720 (some with tail-looking scanner also); four 20mm each with 500 rounds.

FB.XVIII Dubbed Tse-Tse Fly, this multi-role Coastal Command fighter had low-blown engines and carried a 57mm six-pounder Molins gun with 25 rounds plus four Brownings, as well as eight 60lb rockets or bombs.

NF.XIX Mk XIII developed with AI.VIII or X or SCR.720 in bulged Universal Nose and low-blown Merlin 25s.

B.XX Canadian-built B.IV (USAAF designation F-8).

FB.21 to T.29, Canadian marks with Packard V-1650 (Merlin) engines, not all built.

NF.30 Night fighter with two-stage engines, paddle blades, AI Mk X and various sensing, spoofing or jamming avionics, based on Mk XIX.

PR.32 Extended-span reconnaissance version with Merlin 113/114.

Mk 33 First Royal Navy Sea Mosquito version, with power-folding wings, oleo main legs (in place of rubber in compression), low-blown engines driving four-blade propellers, arrester hook, four 20mm cannon, torpedo (or various bomb/rocket loads), American ASH radar and rocket JATO boost.

PR.34 Strategic reconnaissance version, with 113/114 engines, extra-bulged belly for 1,269 gal fuel (200gal drop tanks) and pressure cabin.

B.35 Equivalent bomber version, with PR and target-tug offshoots.

NF.36 Postwar fighter, with 113/114 engines and AI Mk X.

TF.37 Naval torpedo-fighter; basically Mk 33 with AI/ASV Mk XIII.

NF.38 Final fighter, mainly exported; AI Mk IX, forward cockpit.

TT.39 Complete rebuild by General Aircraft as specialised target tug

FB.40 Australian-built Mk VI, with PR.40 as conversions.

PR.41 Australian-built derivative of PR.IX and Mk 40.

T.43 Australian trainer; all Australian production had Packard engines.

Fairey Firefly
Firefly I to 7 and U.8 to 10

Origin: The Fairey Aviation Company.

Type: Originally two-seat naval fighter; later, see text.

Engine: I, up to No 470, one 1,730hp Rolls-Royce Griffon IIB vee-12 liquid-cooled; from No 471, 1,990hp Griffon XII; Mks 4–7, 2,245hp Griffon 74.

Dimensions: Span (I-III) 44ft 6in (13·55m), (4-6) 41ft 2in (12·55m), (7) 44ft 6in (13·55m); length (I-III) 37ft 7in (11·4m); (4-6) 37ft 11in (11·56m); (7) 38ft 3in (11·65m); height (I-III) 13ft 7in (4·15m); (4-7) 14ft 4in (4·37m).

Weights: Empty (I) 9,750lb (4422kg); (4) 9,900lb (4491kg); (7) 11,016lb (4997kg); loaded (I) 14,020lb (6359kg); (4) 13,927lb (6317kg) clean, 16,096lb (7301kg) with external stores; (7) 13,970lb (6337kg).

Performance: Maximum speed (I) 316mph (509km/h); (4) 386mph (618km/h); initial climb (I) 1,700ft (518m)/min; (4) 2,050ft (625m)/min; service ceiling (I) 28,000ft (8534m); (4) 31,000ft (9450m); range on internal fuel (I) 580 miles (933km); (4) 760 miles (1223km).

Armament: (I) four fixed 20mm Hispano cannon in wings; underwing racks for up to 2,000lb (907kg) of weapons or other stores; (4 and 5) usually similar to I in most sub-types; (6) no guns, but underwing load increased to 3,000lb and varied; (7) no guns, but underwing load remained at 3,000lb and equipment changed.

History: First flight 22 December 1941; first production F.I 26 August 1942; production FR.4, 25 May 1945; final delivery of new aircraft May 1955.

User: UK (RN); other countries post-war.

Development: Before World War II Fairey designed a light bomber, P.4/34, from which evolved the Fulmar naval two-seat fighter to Specification O.8/38. A total of 600 of these slender carrier-based aircraft served during the war with various equipment and roles. The Firefly followed the same formula, but was much more powerful and useful. Designed to N.5/40 — a merger of N.8/39 and N.9/39 — it was a clean stressed-skin machine with folding elliptical wings housing the four cannon and with the trailing edge provided with patented Youngman flaps for use at low speeds

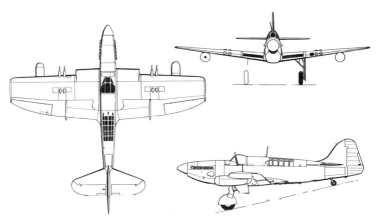

Above: The FR.5 was one of many post-war variants.

and in cruise. Unlike the installation on the Barracuda, these flaps could be recessed into the wing. The pilot sat over the leading edge, with the observer behind the wing. The main wartime version was the Mk I, widely used from the end of 1943 in all theatres. Fairey and General Aircraft built 429 F.Is, 376 FR.Is with ASH radar and then 37 NF.2 night fighters. There followed the more powerful Mk III, from which derived the redesigned FR.4 with two-stage Griffon and wing-root radiators. There were 160 of these, 40 going to the Netherlands and the rest serving in Korea, with the 352 Mk 5s with folding wings. There were FR, NF and AS (anti-submarine) Mk 5s, and they were followed by the 133 specialised AS.6 versions with all role equipment tailored to anti-submarine operations. The 151 AS.7s rounded off production, this being a redesigned three-seater, with new tail and wings and distinctive beard radiator. More than 400 Fireflies were rebuilt in the 1950s as two-cockpit T.1s or armed T.2s, or as various remotely piloted drone versions (U.8, U.9, U.10). Some were converted as target tugs and for other civil duties.

Below: Deck parties aboard fleet carrier (probably *Illustrious*) fold the wings of a Firefly I after an attack on Japanese installations. Some aircraft were fitted with underwing rocket rails.

Fairey Fulmar
Fulmar I and II

Origin: Fairey Aviation Co, Hayes.
Type: Carrier fighter bomber.
Engine: (I) 1,080hp Rolls-Royce Merlin VIII vee-12 liquid-cooled; (II) 1,300hp Merlin 30.
Dimensions: Span 46ft 4½in (14·14m); length 40ft 2in (12·24m); height 10ft 8in (3·25m).
Weights: Empty (II) 7,015lb (3182kg); normal loaded (II) 9,672lb (4387kg); maximum 10,200lb (4627kg).
Performance: Maximum speed (II) 272mph (440km/h); service ceiling (II) 27,200ft (8300m); range 780 miles (1255km).
Armament: Eight 0.303in or (some aircraft) four 0.5in Browning fixed in outer wings (some also 0.303in Vickers K manually aimed from rear cockpit), with underwing racks for two 250lb (113kg) bombs.
History: First flight 4 January 1940; service delivery 10 May 1940.
User: UK (RN).

Development: Based on the P.4/34 light bomber first flown in January 1937, the Fulmar was designed by a team under Marcel O. Lobelle to meet the Admiralty's urgent need for a modern shipboard fighter. Specification O.8/38 was drawn up around the Fairey design, stipulating eight guns and a seat for a navigator. Development and clearance for service was amazingly rapid, and 806 Sqn equipped with the new fighter in July, reaching the Mediterranean aboard *Illustrious* in August 1940. Later 14 FAA squadrons used the Fulmar, most seeing intensive action in the Mediterranean or aboard CAM (catapult-armed merchant) ships in Atlantic convoys (a Fulmar was shot from a CAM ship as early as August 1941). Against the Regia Aeronautica the Fulmar did well, having adequate performance, good handling and fair endurance. After building 250 Mk I Fairey delivered 350 of the more powerful Mk II, the last in February 1943.

Above: A standard Fairey Fulmar I (eight 0.303in guns).

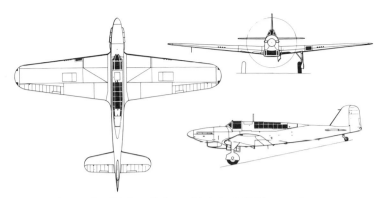

Above: N1858, the fifth Fulmar I. The prototype, N1854, flew in January 1940, and a production Fulmar was delivered in May.

Below: A superb photograph of a Fulmar I landing along the port (left) side of the deck of a fleet carrier in November 1940.

Gloster Gladiator

S.S.37 Gladiator I and II and Sea Gladiator

Origin: Gloster Aircraft Company.
Type: Single-seat fighter; (Sea Gladiator) carrier-based fighter.
Engine: One 840hp Bristol Mercury IX or IXS nine-cylinder radial; (Gladiator II) usually Mercury VIIIA of similar power.
Dimensions: Span 32ft 3in (9·85m); length 27ft 5in (8·38m); height 10ft 4in (3·17m).
Weights: Empty 3,450lb (1565kg); (Sea Gladiator) 3,745lb; loaded 4,750lb (2155kg); (Sea Gladiator) 5,420lb.
Performance: Maximum speed 253mph (407km/h); (Sea Gladiator) 245mph; initial climb 2,300ft (700m)/min; service ceiling 33,000ft (10,060m); range 440 miles (708km); (Sea Gladiator) 425 miles.
Armament: First 71 aircraft, two 0·303in Vickers in fuselage, one 0·303in Lewis under each lower wing; subsequent, four 0·303in Brownings in same locations, fuselage guns with 600 rounds and wing guns with 400.
History: First flight (S.S.37) September 1934; (Gladiator I) June 1936; (Sea Gladiator) 1938; service delivery March 1937; final delivery April 1940.
Users: Belgium, China, Egypt, Finland, Greece, Iraq, Ireland, Latvia, Lithuania, Norway, Portugal, South Africa, Sweden, UK (RAF, RN).

Development: Air Ministry Specification F.7/30 recognised that future fighters would have to be faster and better armed, but the delay in placing an order extended to a disgraceful 4½ years, by which time war clouds were distantly gathering and the fabric-covered biplane was swiftly to be judged obsolete. Folland's S.S.37 was built as a very late entrant, long after the competition to F.7/30 ought to have been settled. Though less radical than most contenders it was eventually judged best and, as the Gladiator, was at last ordered in July 1935. Features included neat single-bay wings, each of the four planes having small hydraulically depressed drag flaps; cantilever landing gear with Dowty internally sprung wheels; four guns; and, in the production aircraft, a sliding cockpit canopy. Most early production had the Watts wooden propeller, though performance was better with the three-blade metal Fairey-Reed type. The Mk II aircraft introduced desert filters, auto mixture control and electric starter from internal battery. The Sea Gladiator had full carrier equipment and a dinghy. Total production amounted to at least 767, including 480 for the RAF, 60 Sea Gladiators and

Right: This Gladiator I, seen in service with No 73 Sqn just before the war, was one of the second production batch, K7892-8077. K7939 was the first to be fitted with the Browning gun in place of the Vickers/ Lewis combination. All this batch had the Watts propeller, very like that fitted to the pre-1940 Hurricane I. Sea Gladiators could be distinguished by the belly dinghy fairing.

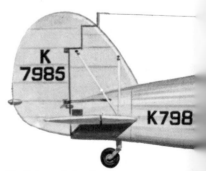

216 exported to 12 foreign countries. Gladiators of the Auxiliary Air Force intercepted the first bombing raid on Britain, over the Firth of Forth in September 1939, and these highly manoeuvrable biplanes were constantly in heroic action for the next three years. Aircraft from the torpedoed *Glorious* operated from a frozen lake in Norway and three Sea Gladiators defended Malta against the Regia Aeronautica from 11 June 1940.

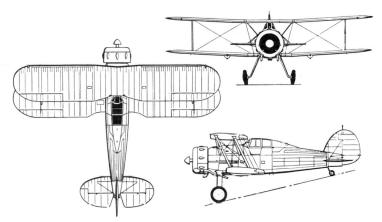

Above: Gloster Gladiator I (Mk II almost identical).

Below: This Gladiator destined for Latvia was one of 14 export versions, some of which saw action during World War II.

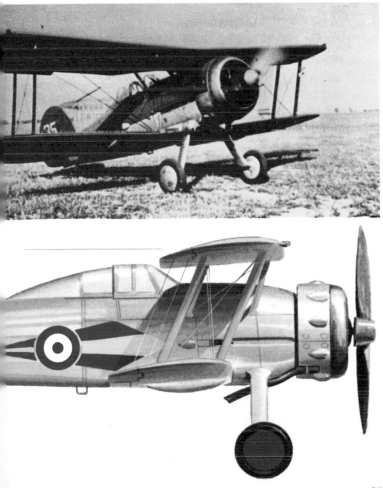

Gloster G.41 Meteor

G.41 Meteor I and III

Origin: Gloster Aircraft Company; (post-war, other builders).
Type: Single-seat fighter.
Engines: Two Rolls-Royce centrifugal turbojets (sub-types, see text).
Dimensions: Span 43ft 0in (13·1m); length 41ft 4in (12·6m); height 13ft 0in (3·96m).
Weights: Empty 8,140lb (3693kg); loaded 13,800lb (6260kg).
Performance: Maximum speed (I) 410mph (660km/h); initial climb (I) 2,155ft (657m)/min; service ceiling 40,000–44,000ft (12,192–13,410m); range on internal fuel about 1,000 miles at altitude (1610km).
Armament: Four 20mm Hispano cannon on sides of nose.
History: First flight (prototype) 5 March 1943; squadron delivery (F.I) 12 July 1944.
Users: UK (RAF), US (AAF, one, on exchange); (post-war, many air forces).

Development: Designed to Specification F.9/40 by George Carter, the Gloster G.41 was to have been named Thunderbolt, but when this name was given to the P-47 the Gloster twin-jet became the Meteor. The first Allied jet combat design, it was surprisingly large, with generous wing area. Though this made the early marks poor performers even on two engines, it proved beneficial in the long term, because marvellous engine development by Rolls-Royce transformed the Meteor into a multi-role aircraft with outstanding speed, acceleration and climb and, thanks to its ample proportions, it could be developed for such challenging roles as advanced dual training, long-range reconnaissance and two-seat night fighting. Initial development was protracted, not because of the revolutionary engines but because of the ailerons, tail and nosewheel. Several engines were used. First flight was with two Halford H.1, later called de Havilland Goblin; second, on 12 June 1943, was with Rolls-Royce Welland (W.2B/23); third, on 13 November 1943, was with Metrovick F.2 axials. The Welland, rated at 1,700lb, was chosen for the first batch of 16 Meteor Is, which entered service on 12 July 1944 with one flight of 616 Sqn, the pilots having previously converted. This was eight days before the first nine Me 262s of KG51 entered service. The first task of the new jet was to chase flying bombs, and even the Meteor I soon showed that it was formidable (though the guns jammed on the first encounter and F/O Dean finally succeeded by daringly tipping the missile over with his wing tip). The first major production version was the F.III, with 2,000lb Derwent 1s, extra tankage, sliding canopy and, on the last 15, longer nacelles. The Mk 4 introduced the redesigned Derwent 5 of 3,500lb thrust, with bigger nacelles on a wing whose tips were clipped to improve speed and rate of roll. In 1945 a Mk 4 set a world speed record at 606mph, raised the following year to 616mph. There were many post-war versions.

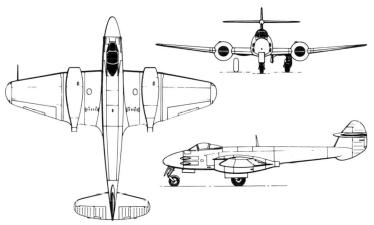

Above: Gloster Meteor F.III (Welland or Derwent engines similar).

Below left: An original Meteor F.I fighter with 616 Sqn in July 1944. Provision was made for six cannon, two being omitted.

Below: The Meteor F.III is distinguished from the F.I by its neat sliding canopy. From No 15 (EE245) the engine was the Derwent.

Hawker Hurricane

Hurricane I to XII, Sea Hurricane IA to XIIA

Origin: Hawker Aircraft Ltd; also built by Gloster Aircraft, SABCA (Belgium) and Canadian Car & Foundry Inc.

Type: Single-seat fighter; later, fighter-bomber, tank buster and ship-based fighter.

Engine: One Rolls-Royce Merlin vee-12 liquid-cooled (see text for sub-types).

Dimensions: Span 40ft (12·19m); length 32ft (9·75m); (Mk I) 31ft 5in; (Sea Hurricanes) 32ft 3in; height 13ft 1in (4m).

Weights: Empty (I) 4,670lb (2118kg); (IIA) 5,150lb (2335kg); (IIC) 5,640lb (2558kg); (IID) 5,800lb (2631kg); (IV) 5,550lb (2515kg); (Sea H.IIC) 5,788lb (2625kg); loaded (I) 6,600lb (2994kg); (IIA) 8,050lb (3650kg); (IIC) 8,250lb (3742kg); (IID) 8,200lb (3719kg); (IV) 8,450lb (3832kg); (Sea H. IIC) 8,100lb (3674kg).

Performance: Maximum speed (I) 318mph (511km/h); (IIA, B, C) 345–335mph (560–540km/h); (IID) 286mph (460km/h); (IV) 330mph (531km/h); (Sea H. IIC) 342mph (550km/h); initial climb (I) 2,520ft (770m)/min; (IIA) 3,150ft (960m)/min; (rest, typical) 2,700ft (825m)/min; service ceiling (I) 36,000ft (10.973m); (IIA) 41,000ft (12,500m); (rest, typical) 34,000ft (10,365m); range (all, typical) 460 miles (740km), or with two 44 Imp gal drop tanks 950 miles (1530km).

Armament: (I) eight 0·303in Brownings, each with 333 rounds (Belgian model, four 0·5in FN-Brownings); (IIA) same, with provision for 12 guns and two 250lb bombs; (IIB) 12 Brownings and two 250 or 500lb bombs; (IIC) four 20mm Hispano cannon and bombs; (IID) two 40mm Vickers S guns and two 0·303in Brownings; (IV) universal wing with two Brownings and two Vickers S, two 500lb bombs, eight rockets, smoke installation or other stores.

History: First flight (prototype) 6 November 1935; (production Mk I) 12 October 1937; (II) 11 June 1940; (Canadian Mk X) January 1940; final delivery September 1944.

Users: (Wartime) Australia, Belgium, Canada, Czechoslovakia, Egypt, Finland, India, Iran, Iraq, Ireland, Jugoslavia, New Zealand, Poland, Portugal, Romania, South Africa, Soviet Union, Turkey, UK (RAF, RN).

continued ▶

Above: This Mk I, seen in the markings of No 73 Sqn based at Rouviers, France, in 1939, was one of a batch of 500 built by Gloster. P2682 of this batch was the first with the Rotol propeller.

Right: A much later Hurricane, this Mk IIC, HL716, was one of a batch of 388 built in 1942. Note Vokes filter, drop tanks and Pacific-area markings.

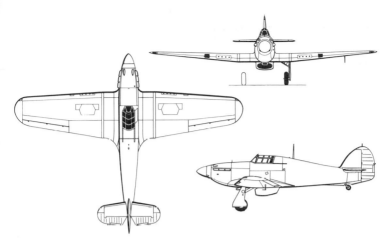

Above: Hawker Hurricane I with stressed-skin wings.

Above: The original Hawker F.36/34 prototype,
flying from Brooklands in 1935. Obvious
changes to produce the Hurricane included
removal of the tailplane strut and addition of
the rear underfin, radio and guns, but in fact
the largest modification was redesign of the
engine installation because of a major change
in the Merlin. The official title of K5083 was
Hawker High-Speed Monoplane.

Development: Until well into 1941 the Hurricane was by far the most numerous of the RAF's combat aircraft and it bore the brunt of the early combats with the Luftwaffe over France and Britain. Designed by Camm as a Fury Monoplane, with Goshawk engine and spatted landing gear, it was altered on the drawing board to have the more powerful PV.12 (Merlin) and inwards-retracting gear and, later, to have not four machine guns but the unprecedented total of eight. The Air Ministry wrote Specification F.36/34 around it and after tests with the prototype ordered the then-fantastic total of 600 in June 1936. In September 1939 the 497 delivered equipped 18 squadrons and by 7 August 1940 no fewer than 2,309 had been delivered, compared with 1,383 Spitfires, equipping 32 squadrons, compared with $18\frac{1}{2}$ Spitfire squadrons. Gloster's output in 1940 was 130 per month. By this time the Hurricane I was in service with new metal-skinned wings, instead of fabric, and three-blade variable pitch (later constant-speed) propeller instead of the wooden Watts two-blader. In the hectic days of 1940 the Hurricane was found to be an ideal bomber destroyer, with steady sighting and devastating cone of fire; turn radius was better than that of any other ▶

Below: Belgian MK I (armament, four 0.5in FN Browning) of 2 Esc "Le Chardon" of Regiment I/2 at Diest, 1940.

Above: Pilots of No 257 Sqn
race over a snowy
Martlesham Heath towards
their Hurricanes in early
1941.

Below: An idyllic study of
a Hurricane I (one of a
batch of 600 built by
Gloster) with two Spitfire
IIs from a batch of 1,000
built at Castle Bromwich,
all with an Operational
Training Unit, 1942.

Above: A Hurricane I for Yugoslavia being factory-tested near Brooklands in early 1939. Many of the Yugoslav Hurricanes saw action against the Luftwaffe in early 1941.

Right: another export customer for this great warplane was Finland, a dozen being sent freely to help in the Winter War in late 1939. Survivors later become Britain's enemies.

Below right: "Last of the Many", the final Hurricane (PZ865, a IIC bomber) delivered in September 1944.

monoplane fighter, but the all-round performance of the Bf 109E was considerably higher. The more powerful Mk II replaced the 1,030hp Merlin II by the 1,280hp Merlin XX and introduced new armament and drop tanks. In North West Europe it became a ground-attack aircraft, and in North Africa a tank-buster with 40mm guns. While operating from merchant-ship catapults and carriers it took part in countless fleet-defence actions, the greatest being the defence of the August 1942 Malta convoy, when 70 Sea Hurricanes fought off more than 600 Axis attackers, destroying 39 for the loss of seven fighters. The Hurricane was increasingly transferred to the Far East, Africa and other theatres, and 2,952 were dispatched to the Soviet Union, some receiving skis. Hurricanes were used for many special trials of armament and novel flight techniques (one having a jettisonable biplane upper wing). Total production amounted to 12,780 in Britain and 1,451 in Canada (after 1941 with Packard Merlins) and many hundreds were exported both before and after World War II.

Above: BE485 was a Mk II bomber built at Langley in 1941. The revelation that the Hurricane could carry bombs was a small fillip to morale at a dark period of the war. At first only the 250-pounder could be carried (as here); later the wing hardpoint took 500-pounders, or eight rockets, drop tanks, SBCs (small bomb containers), 40mm anti-tank guns or smoke apparatus.

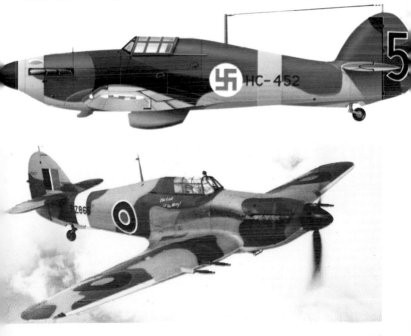

Hawker Tempest

Tempest V and VI

Origin: Hawker Aircraft Ltd; Mk II, Bristol Aeroplane Company.
Type: Single-seat fighter bomber.
Engine: (V) one 2,180hp Napier Sabre II 24-cylinder flat-H sleeve-valve liquid-cooled; (VI) one 2,340hp Sabre V.
Dimensions: Span 41ft (12·5m); length 33ft 8in (10·26m); height 16ft 1in (4·9m).
Weights: Empty 9,100lb (4128kg); loaded 13,500lb (6130kg).
Performance: Maximum speed (V) 427mph (688km/h); (VI) 438mph (704km/h); initial climb 3,000ft (914m)/min; service ceiling, about 37,000ft (11,280m); range (bombs, not tanks) 740 miles (1191km).
Armament: Four 20mm Hispano cannon in outer wings; underwing racks for eight rockets or up to 2,000lb (907kg) bombs.
History: First flight (prototype Mk V) 2 September 1942; (Mk I) 24 February 1943; (production V) 21 June 1943; (Mk II) 28 June 1943; (prototype VI) 9 May 1944; (production II) 4 October 1944.
Users: New Zealand, UK (RAF).

Development: The Typhoon was noted for its thick wing — occasional erratic flight behaviour at high speeds was traced to compressibility (local airflow exceeding the speed of sound), which had never before been encountered. In 1940 Hawker schemed a new laminar-flow wing with a root thickness five inches less and an elliptic planform rather like a Spitfire. This was used on the Typhoon II, ordered in November 1941 to Specification F.10/41, but there were so many changes the fighter was renamed Tempest. Fuel had to be moved from the thinner wing to the fuselage, making the latter longer, and a dorsal fin was added. The short-barrel Mk V guns were buried in the wing. Though the new airframe could take the promising Centaurus engine it was the Sabre-engined Mk V that was produced first, reaching the Newchurch Wing in time to destroy 638 out of the RAF's total of 1,771 flying bombs shot down in the summer of 1944. After building 800 Mk Vs Hawker turned out 142 of the more powerful Mk VI type with bigger radiator and oil coolers in the leading edge. After much delay, with production assigned first to Gloster and then to Bristol, the Centaurus-powered Mk II — much quieter and nicer to fly — entered service in November 1945, and thus missed the war. A few Mks 5 and 6 (post-war designations) were converted as target tugs.

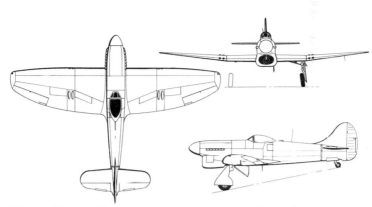

Above: Hawker Tempest V, the first version in service.

Above: The first production Tempest, JN729 (a Mk V, Series 1) on test from Langley, near Slough. It first flew in June 1943, but by now its wing has become well scuffed by boots and the fuselage blackened by exhaust.

Left: NV768 was built as a Mk V Series 2, and then modified with wing-root oil coolers like a MkVI and used for experiments with annular radiators and even giant ducted spinners.

Hawker Typhoon

Typhoon IA and IB

Origin: Hawker Aircraft Ltd; built by Gloster Aircraft Company.
Type: Single-seat fighter bomber.
Engine: (Production IB) one 2,180hp Napier Sabre II, 24-cylinder flat-H sleeve-valve liquid-cooled.
Dimensions: Span 41ft 7in (12·67m); length 31ft 11in (9·73m); height 15ft 3½in (4·66m).
Weights: Empty 8,800lb (3992kg); loaded 13,250lb (6010kg).
Performance: Maximum speed 412mph (664km/h); initial climb 3,000ft (914m)/min; service ceiling 35,200ft (10,730m); range (with bombs) 510 miles (821km), (with drop tanks) 980 miles (1577km).
Armament: (IA) 12 0·303in Brownings (none delivered); (IB) four 20mm Hispano cannon in outer wings, and racks for eight rockets or two 500lb (227kg) (later 1,000lb, 454kg) bombs.
History: First flight (Tornado) October 1939; (Typhoon) 24 February 1940; (production Typhoon) 27 May 1941; final delivery November 1945.
Users: Canada, New Zealand, UK (RAF).

Development: The Typhoon's early life was almost total disaster. Though the concept of so big and powerful a combat aircraft was bold and significant, expressed in Specification F.18/37, the Griffon and Centaurus engines were ignored and reliance was placed on the complex and untried Vulture and Sabre. The former powered the R-type fighter, later named Tornado, which ground to a halt with abandonment of the Vulture in early 1941. The N-type (Napier), named Typhoon, was held back six months by the desperate need for Hurricanes. Eventually, after most painful development, production began at Gloster Aircraft in 1941 and Nos 56 and 609 Sqns at Duxford began to re-equip with the big bluff-looking machine in September of that year. But the Sabre was unreliable, rate of climb and performance at height were disappointing and the rear fuselage persisted in coming apart.

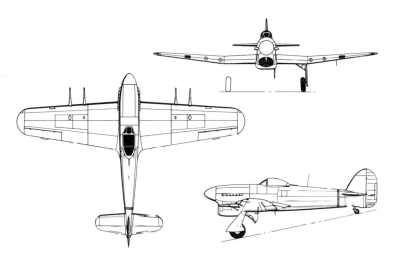

Above: Hawker Typhoon IB with sliding canopy and whip aerial.

There was much talk of scrapping the programme, but, fortunately for the Allies, the snags were gradually overcome. In November 1942 the Typhoon suddenly sprang to favour by demonstrating it could catch and destroy the fastest fighter-bombers in the Luftwaffe which were making low-level hit-and run raids. In 1943 "Tiffy" squadrons shot up and blasted everything that moved in northern France and the Low Countries, and in the summer of 1944 the hundreds of Typhoons — by now thoroughly proven and capable of round-the-clock operation from rough forward strips — formed the backbone of 2nd Tactical Air Force attack strength, sending millions of cannon shells, rockets and heavy bombs into German ground forces and in a single day knocking out 175 tanks in the Falaise gap. Gloster built 3,315 of the 3,330 Typhoons, the final 3,000-odd having a clear bubble hood instead of a heavy-framed cockpit with a car-type door on each side. ▶

Above left: MN304 was one of a batch of 800 Mk IBs (all of them made by Gloster) with sliding canopy, faired guns (like all Typhoons depicted here) and rocket rails. The serial is repeated in white on the fin.

Above: JP853, an early Mk IB.

Left: An early MK IB, seen bombed-up, with 198 Sqn, based at Martragny, France, July 1944.

Above: JR128 came earlier in a production batch of 600 than JR371, illustrated on the previous page, yet it has the later type of canopy (a vast improvement inspired by the canopy of the Fw 190). Final batches of Typhoons had four-blade propellers.

Right: In an exceptional blast-proof dispersal, a Mk IB of 175 Sqn is serviced between flights and bombed up with 500-pounders. The photograph was probably taken in 1943, long before the use of D-Day "invasion stripes" which appeared on 5 June 1944 on all Allied combat aircraft. The Typhoon was thought to be easily mistaken for an Fw 190, and so was adorned with black and white stripes!

Supermarine Spitfire and Seafire

Mks I to 24 and Seafire I, III, XV, XVII and 45-47

Origin: Supermarine Aviation Works (Vickers) Ltd; also built by Vickers-Armstrongs, Castle Bromwich, and Westland Aircraft; (Seafire) Cunliffe-Owen Aircraft and Westland.

Type: Single-seat fighter, fighter-bomber or reconnaissance; (Seafire) carrier-based fighter.

Engine: One Rolls-Royce Merlin or Griffon vee-12 liquid-cooled (see text).

Dimensions: Span 36ft 10in (11·23m), clipped, 32ft 2in, or, more often, 32ft 7in (9·93m), extended, 40ft 2in (12·24m); length 29ft 11in (9·12m), later, with two-stage engine, typically 31ft 3½in (9·54m), Griffon engine, typically 32ft 8in (9·96m), final (eg Seafire 47) 34ft 4in (10·46m); height 11ft 5in (3·48m), with Griffon, typically 12ft 9in (3·89m).

Weights: Empty (Mk I) 4,810lb (2182kg); (IX) 5,610lb (2545kg); (XIV) 6,700lb (3040kg); (Sea.47) 7,625lb (3458kg); maximum loaded (I) 5,784lb (2624kg); (IX) 9,500lb (4310kg); (XIV) 10,280lb (4663kg); Sea.47 12,750lb (5784kg).

Performance: Maximum speed (I) 355–362mph (580km/h); (IX) 408mph (657km/h); (XIV) 448mph (721km/h); (Sea.47) 451mph (724km/h); initial climb (I) 2,530ft (770m)/min; (IX) 4,100ft (1250m)/min; (XIV) 4,580ft (1396m)/min; (Sea.47) 4,800ft (1463m)/min; range on internal fuel (I) 395 miles (637km); (IX) 434 miles (700km); (XIV) 460 miles (740km); (Sea.47) 405 miles (652km).

Armament: See "Development" text.

History: First flight (prototype) 5 March 1936; (production Mk I) July 1938; final delivery (Mk 24) October 1947.

Users: (Wartime) Australia, Canada, Czechoslovakia, Egypt, France, Italy (CB), Jugoslavia, Netherlands, Norway, Poland, Portugal, South Africa, Soviet Union, Turkey, UK (RAF, RN), US (AAF).

Development: Possibly the most famous combat aircraft in history, the Spitfire was designed by the dying Reginald Mitchell to Specification F.37/34 using the new Rolls-Royce PV.12 engine later named Merlin. It was the first all-metal stressed-skin fighter to go into production in Britain. The following were main versions.

I Initial version, 450 ordered in June 1936 with 1,030hp Merlin II, two-blade fixed-pitch propeller and four 0·303in Browning guns. Later Mk IA with eight guns, bulged canopy and three-blade DH v-p propeller and Mk IB with two 20mm Hispano and four 0·303. Production: 1,566.

II Mk I built at Castle Bromwich with 1,175hp Merlin XII and Rotol propeller. Production: 750 IIA (eight 0·303), 170 IIB (two 20mm, four 0·303).

III Single experimental model; strengthened Mk I with many changes.

Below: This Mk IIA, flown by S/L Don Finlay, CO of 41 Sqn at Hornchurch in 1940, was the gift of members of the ROC.

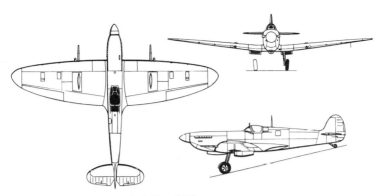

Above: Supermarine Spitfire F.IX.

IV Confusing because Mk IV was first Griffon-engined, one built. Then unarmed Merlin photo-reconnaissance Mk IV delivered in quantity. Production: 229.

V Like PR.IV powered by 1,440hp Merlin 45, many detail changes, main fighter version 1941–42 in three forms: VA, eight 0·303; VB, two 20mm and four 0·303; VC "universal" wing with choice of guns plus two 250lb (113kg) bombs. All with centreline rack for 500lb (227kg) bomb or tank. Many with clipped wings and/or tropical filter under nose. Production: VA, 94; VB, 3,923; VC, 2,447.

VI High-altitude interim interceptor, 1,415hp Merlin 47, pressurised cockpit, two 20mm and four 0·303. Production: 100. *continued* ▶

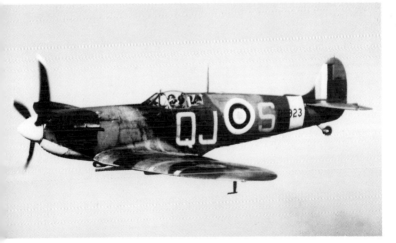

Above: Basically tougher and more powerful than the Mks I and II, the V was the standard version in production in 1941. More were built (6,464) than any other single mark. R6923 was one of many built as a Mk I and converted to a VB. It went to the first user of this mark, 92 Sqn, in March 1941. Below about 15,000 feet it could hold its own, but the Fw 190 was so superior at altitude that the Spitfire IX had hurriedly to be produced, mating the two-stage Merlin with the Mk V airframe.

Above: BL479 was a Spitfire LF.VB, with clipped wings which, with the low-blown Merlin 45 or 50 series engine, produced a fighter mediocre above 20,000 feet but formidable at low level. It was one of a batch of 1,000 built at Castle Bromwich in 1941.

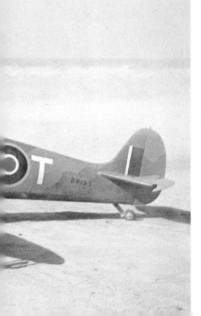

Left: BR195 was one of more than 2,000 Mk V series to be tropicalised by the addition of a Vokes sand filter. The basic Mk V was not particularly sprightly, and with the filter became slower than any mark except the early Seafires. These Spits are seen with 417 Sqn RCAF in Sicily in 1943. They are Mk VCs with the universal wing able to carry any armament fit or various loads of external stores (but the only drop-tank location was on the centreline).

57

VII High-altitude, extended wing-tips, new 1,660hp Merlin 61 with two-stage supercharger (and symmetrical underwing radiators); retractable tailwheel, later broad and pointed rudder. Pressurised cockpit. Production: 140.

VIII Followed interim Mk IX, virtually unpressurised Mk VII in LF (low-altitude, clipped), F (standard) and HF (high-altitude, extended) versions. Production: 1,658.

IX Urgent version to counter Fw 190, quick lash-up of V with Merlin 61; again LF, F and HF versions, plus IXE with two 20mm and two 0·5in. Production: 5,665.

X Pressurised photo-reconnaissance, Merlin 77, whole leading edge forming fuel tank. Production: 16.

XI As X but unpressurised, 1,760hp Merlin 63A or 1,655hp Merlin 70. Mainstay of Photo Reconnaissance Unit 1943–45. Production: 471.

XII Low altitude to counter Fw 190 hit-and-run bomber, 1,735hp Griffon III or IV, strengthened VC or VIII airframe, clipped. Production: 100.

XIII Low-level reconnaissance, low-rated 1,620hp Merlin 32, four 0·303. Production: 16.

XIV First with two-stage Griffon, 2,050hp Mk 65 with deep symmetric radiators and five-blade propeller, completely redesigned airframe with new fuselage, broad fin/rudder, inboard ailerons, retractable tailwheel. F.XIV, two 20mm and four 0·303; F.XIVE, two 20mm and two 0·5in; FR.XIVE, same guns, cut-down rear fuselage and teardrop hood, clipped wings, F.24 camera and extra fuel. Active in 1944, destroyed over 300 flying bombs. Production: 957.

XVI As Mk IX but 1,705hp Packard Merlin 266; LF.IXE, E-guns and clipped, many with teardrop hood, extra fuel. Production: 1,054.

XVIII Definitive wartime fighter derived from interim XIV, extra fuel, stronger, F and FR versions, some of latter even more fuel and tropical equipment. Production: 300.

XIX Final photo-reconnaissance, 2,050hp Griffon 65 and unpressurised, then Griffon 66 with pressure cabin and increased wing tankage; both option of deep slipper tank for 1,800 mile (2900km) range. Made last RAF Spitfire sortie, Malaya, 1 April 1954. Production: 225.

21 Post-war, redesigned aircraft with different structure and shape, 2,050hp Griffon 65 or 85, four 20mm and 1,000lb (454kg) bombs. Production: 122.

22 Bubble hood, 24-volt electrics, some with 2,375hp Griffon 65 and contraprop. Production: 278.

24 Redesigned tail, short-barrel cannon, zero-length rocket launchers. Production: 54. Total Spitfire production 20,334.

Seafire IB Navalised Spitfire VB, usually 1,415hp low-rated Merlin 46. Fixed wings but hook and slinging points. Conversions: 166.

IIC Catapult spools, strengthened landing gear, 1,645hp Merlin 32 and four-blade propeller. Various sub-types, Universal wing. Production: 262 Supermarine, 110 Westland.

III Manual double-fold wing, 1,585hp Merlin 55M, various versions. Production: 870 Westland, 350 Cunliffe-Owen.

XV (Later F.15) 1,850hp Griffon VI, four-blade, asymmetric radiators, cross between Seafire III and Spitfire XII. Production: 390.

XVII (F.17) Increased fuel, cut-down fuselage and bubble hood. Production: (cut by war's end): 232.

45 New aircraft entirely, corresponding to Spitfire 21; Griffon 61 (five-blade) or 85 (contraprop); fixed wing, four 20mm. Production: 50.

46 Bubble hood like Spitfire 22. Production: 24.

47 Navalised Spitfire 24, hydraulically folding wings, carb-air intake just behind propeller, increased fuel. Fought in Malaya and Korea. Production: 140. Total Seafires: 2,556.

Left: When the Mk IB and IIB appeared with two 20mm Hispanos the fact was obvious to German pilots from the long faired barrels and the blisters over the ammunition drums. They found the Mk IX, however, hard to tell from a Mk V at a distance, and from 1942 had to respect all Spitfires due to the Merlin 61.

Below: Post-war models included the F.21 (LA217) and F.22 (PK312).

Westland Whirlwind

Whirlwind I, IA

Origin: Westland Aircraft Ltd.
Type: Single-seat day fighter (later fighter-bomber).
Engines: Two 885hp Rolls-Royce Peregrine I vee-12 liquid-cooled.
Dimensions: Span 45ft (13·72m); length 32ft 9in (9·98m); height 11ft 7in (3·52m).
Weights: Empty (I) 7,840lb (3699kg); (IA) 8,310lb (3770kg); maximum loaded 10,270lb (4658kg); (IA) 11,388lb (5166kg).
Performance: Maximum speed (clean) 360mph (580km/h), (with bombs) 270mph (435km/h); initial climb (clean) 3,000ft (915m)/min; service ceiling (clean) 30,000ft (9144m); range, not recorded but about 800 miles (1290km).
Armament: Standard, four 20mm Hispano Mk I cannon in nose, each with 60-round drum; IA added underwing racks for bomb load up to 1,000lb (454kg).
History: First flight 11 October 1938; service delivery June 1940; final delivery December 1941.
User: UK (RAF).

Development: At the outbreak of World War II the gravest deficiency of the RAF was in the field of twin-engined high-performance machines for use as long-range escort or night fighters. This was precisely the mission of

Below: Though flown in 1938 the distinctive Whirlwind was kept secret from the British public for nearly four years, though it was known to be included in Luftwaffe recognition handbooks in 1940. This Mk I was operated from Exeter by 263 Sqn in 1941, occasionally venturing on ''Rhubarb'' offensive sweeps over France.

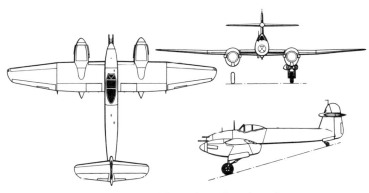

Above: Westland Whirlwind I, without bomb racks.

the Whirlwind, designed to a specification as early as F.37/35. It was a fine and pleasant machine, and in its slender nose was an unprecedented punch. Yet its development was delayed by engine troubles, the Peregrine being an unhappy outgrowth of the reliable Kestrel; another trouble was that, despite Fowler flaps, the landing speed was 80mph which was incompatible with short grass fields. Eventually only 263 and 137 Sqns used the type, which in combat showed much promise. In August 1941 No 263 escorted Blenheims to Cologne in daylight! Only 112 were built, ending their days as "Whirlibombers" on cross-Channel "Rhubarb" sorties strafing and bombing targets of opportunity.

Below: Specification F.37/35 did not stipulate use of two engines but it did call for armament of four 20mm cannon. At the time this was a tremendous armament, and it was most successfully carried into effect by the Westland company. The Achilles heel of the Whirlwind was its weak and unreliable engine. With Merlins it could have been a real world-beater, especially with handed propellers. With Peregrines it was useless, and the last 88 of the 200 ordered were cancelled. Their only effective use was as bombers, after conversion in late 1941.

SOVIET UNION

When Hitler's terrible war machine was unleashed against the USSR on 22 June 1941 the plan was to wipe out almost all the Red Army and VVS (air force) in a matter of weeks. The plan almost came off; even the Russians admitted the loss of over 1,200 aircraft in the first nine hours, and after a week more than 90 per cent of the Soviet front-line strength had ceased to exist.

So secretive had the Russians been that the world learned of their aircraft from pictures put out by the Germans. The only two fighters were thought to be the Chato biplane and Rata monoplane, and the names were uncomplimentary ones bestowed by Franco's pilots in Spain! Not until about 1960 did students of Soviet airpower really begin to piece together the impressive story of what had been accomplished by the Soviet OKBs (design bureaus).

Numerically the Chato and Rata (actually the I-15 and I-16) had indeed been the chief fighters in 1941, but much better machines were in production. The LaGGs, MiGs and Yaks were destined to be produced in quantities fantastic by any yardstick, despite the need in the autumn of 1941 to evacuate most of the original plants and set up new production facilities far to the east. Gradually, and at horrific cost, the command of the sky on the Eastern Front was to be wrested from the

The LaGG-3 was one of several indifferent Russian types whose main assets were robustness and simplicity. This one, with an unusual enlarged tail wheel, was captured by the Finns in 1942.

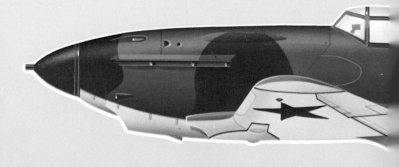

enemy. A small part was played by fighters sent from the USA and Britain, and by non-Russian pilots (notably Poles, Czechs and Frenchmen). It is significant that the élite among these foreign units chose Russian aircraft.

By Western standards the Soviet fighters were crude, small and poorly armed. In fact they were designed with painstaking care, to do the best they could in the harsh environment. In 1941 their structures were wood, because aluminium supplies were far from secure. By 1943 light-alloy primary structure, notably in the wings, had provided more room for fuel. By 1944 airframes were all stressed-skin, and greater power allowed the installation of heavier firepower.

More than 90 per cent of the nearly 70,000 fighters made during World War II to Lavochkin or Yakovlev design had just one cannon and two machine guns. The philosophy was: make fighters small, agile and able to outfly the enemy; what use is firepower if it cannot be brought to bear? A weakness of this argument is that it works well only with experienced pilots. In the Luftwaffe the aces often flew the Bf 109F, with Russian-style armament, and racked up scores topping 200 or even 300. The common herd preferred more guns; and most of the Russian pilots did not last long enough to rise above the common herd.

Lavochkin La-5 and La-7

La-5, -5FN, -7 and -7U

Origin: The design bureau of S. A. Lavochkin.
Type: Single-seat fighter (-7U, dual-control trainer).
Engine: (Original La-5) one 1,330hp Shvetsov M-82A or M-82F 14-cylinder two-row radial; (all other versions) one 1,700hp M-82FN.
Dimensions: Span 32ft 2in (9·8m); length 27ft 10¾in (8·46m); height 9ft 3in (2·84m).
Weights: Empty, no data; loaded (La-5) no data; (La-5FN) 7,406lb (3359kg); (La-7) 7,495lb (3400kg).
Performance: Maximum speed (La-5) 389mph (626km/h); (La-5FN) 403mph (650km/h); (La-7) 423mph (680km/h); initial climb (La-5FN) about 3,600ft (1100m)/min; (La-7) about 3,940ft (1200m)/min; service ceiling (La-5FN) 32,800ft (10,000m); (La-7) 34,448ft (10,500m); range (La-5) 398 miles (640km); (La-5FN) 475 miles (765km); (La-7) 392 miles (630km).
Armament: (La-5, -5FN) two 20mm ShVAK cannon, each with 200 rounds, above engine; optional underwing racks for light bombs up to total of 330lb (150kg); (La-7) three faster-firing ShVAK (one on right, two on left); underwing racks for six RS-82 rockets or two 220lb (100kg) bombs.
History: First flight (re-engined LaGG-3) January 1942; (production La-5) June 1942; (La-5FN) late 1942; (La-7) about June 1943.
User: Soviet Union.

Development: Though the LaGG-3 was a serviceable fighter that used wood rather than scarce light alloys, it was the poorest performer of the new crop of combat aircraft with which the VVS-RKKA (Soviet Military Aviation Defence Forces) sought to halt the German invader. It was natural that urgent consideration should be given to ways of improving it and during 1941 Lavochkin's team converted one LaGG-3 to have an M-82 radial engine. Despite its fractionally greater installed drag (a matter of 1%) it offered speed increased from 353 to 373mph and, in particular, improved all-round performance at height. The liquid-cooled fighter was cancelled in May 1942, all production switching to the new machine, designated LaGG-5. But within a matter of weeks this in turn was replaced on the assembly line by a further improvement, tested as a prototype early in 1942, with a new fuselage ▶

Right: The La-7 was aerodynamically cleaned-up compared with the otherwise similar La-5FN, the most obvious change being relocation of the supercharger duct in the left wing root. This example was Moscow-built, with two ShVAK guns.

Below: Unusual because of its shorter supercharger air inlet duct above the engine, this La-5FN is typical of about 15,000 fighters of this type flown by pilots from at least nine Allied countries.

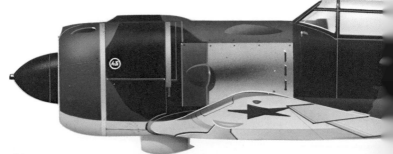

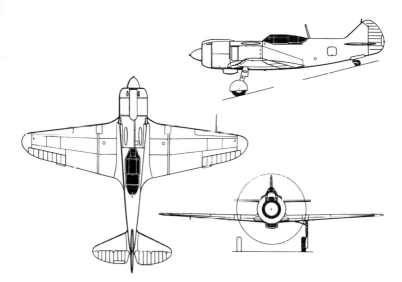

Above: Lavochkin La-5FN with standard twin-ShVAK armament.

containing two 20mm guns and having a lower rear profile behind a canopy giving all-round vision. This was the La-5 which proved to be 28mph faster than a Bf 109G-2 at below 20,000ft. But the German fighter could outclimb it and efforts were made to reduce weight. The resulting La-5FN had an FN (boosted) engine, lighter wing with metal spars and overall weight 379lb (presumably on both empty and gross weight) less. Thousands of -5FNs participated in the huge battles around Kursk and throughout the Eastern front in 1943, demonstrating that Soviet fighters could be more than a match for their opponents. The La-5UTI was a dual trainer. Further refinement led to the harder-hitting La-7, with reduced weight (partly by reducing fuel capacity) and much reduced drag. The -7 and -7U trainer retained the slats and big ailerons that made the Lavochkin fighters such beautiful dog-fighters and were the choice of most of the Soviet aces (Ivan Kozhedub's aircraft is in the Central Soviet Air Force Museum).

Right: A standard La-5FN, distinguished from the La-5 externally by the air duct extended to the front of the engine cowl (the profile drawing on the preceding pages shows an alternative, shorter La-5FN duct unlike that on the original La-5).

Below: Inscribed "In the name of Hero of the Soviet Union Lt-Col N. Koniev", this La-5FN was flown by top-scoring ace Ivan Kozhedub in 1944. Later that year, with 176 IAP, he changed to a white La-7.

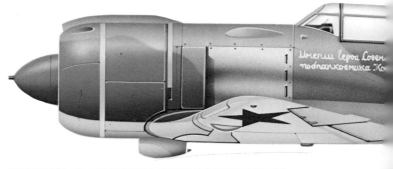

Below: La-5FNs of the 1st Czech (Partisan)
IAP operating from Preborsk in 1943.

Lavochkin LaGG-3

I-22, LaGG-1, I-301, LaGG-3

Origin: The design bureau of S. A. Lavochkin, in partnership with Gorbunov and Gudkov.

Type: Single-seat fighter.

Engine: (-1) one 1,050hp Klimov M-105P (VK-105P) vee-12 liquid-cooled; (-3) one 1,240hp M-105PF with improved propeller.

Dimensions: Span 32ft 2in (9·8m); length 29ft 1¼in (8·9m); height 8ft 10in (3·22m).

Weights: Empty (-1) 5,952lb (2700kg); (-3) 5,764lb (2620kg); maximum loaded (-1) 6,834lb (3100kg); (-3) 7,257lb (3300kg).

Performance: Maximum speed (-1) 373mph (600km/h); (-3) 348mph (560km/h); initial climb (both) 2,953ft (900m)/min; service ceiling (-1) 31,496ft (9600m); (-3) 29,527ft (9000m); range (both) 404 miles (650km).

Armament: Very varied; typically, one 20mm ShVAK firing through propeller hub, with 120 rounds, two 12·7mm BS above engine, each with 220 rounds, and underwing racks for six RS-82 rockets or various light bombs; LaGGs on Il-2 escort had three 12·7mm and two 7·62mm; some had a 23mm VIa cannon and various combinations of machine guns.

History: First flight (I-22) 30 March 1939; (production LaGG-1) late 1940; (production LaGG-3) 1941; final delivery June 1942.

User: Soviet Union.

continued ▶

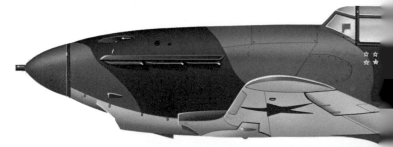

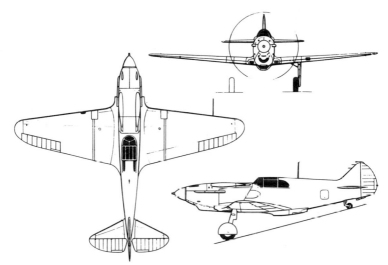

Above: The LaGG-1, which was not fitted with wing slats.

Above: Early LaGG-3 fighters had a prominent horn balance above and below the rudder. This example was operated by an unknown fighter regiment on the Ukrainian front in mid-1942.

Left: A later LaGG with the cleaned-up rudder.

Below: This LaGG-3 was one of those still operational in 1944. It was flown by Yuri Shchipov of 9 IAP, Black Sea Fleet, in the Novorossisk earlier. The lion's head was his personal emblem.

Above: This LaGG-3 had a horn balance at the top of the rudder only. Thickly coated with wax to smooth the exterior, it was flying with the Baltic Fleet when it was shot down over Finland on 6 March 1942. Two-figure numbers were usually the last two digits of the construction number, in this case 070171.

Below: An interesting photograph taken at a winter ceremony at a LaGG-3 regiment. Not only are the aircraft burdened by under-wing RS-82 rockets and 22-GAU (100 litre) drop tanks, but they have ski landing gears which could not retract completely. Performance must have been poor.

Development: Semyon Alekseyevich Lavochkin headed a design committee which included V. P. Gorbunov and M. I. Gudkov in creating the very unusual I-22 fighter prototype of 1938–39. Though outwardly conventional, it was rare among the world's new crop of streamlined monoplane fighters not to have metal stressed-skin construction; instead it was built of wood, except for the control surfaces, which were light alloy with fabric covering, and the flaps which, to avoid damage, were all-metal. The ply skinning was both impregnated and bonded on with phenol-formaldehyde resin, which at the time seemed quaint but today is very widely used for this purpose. The result was a neat, clean and manoeuvrable fighter, which later showed outstanding robustness and resistance to combat damage. On the other hand it was inferior to other Russian fighters in all-round performance. Several hundred had been delivered, as the LaGG-1, when production was switched to the LaGG-3. This had a better engine, leading-edge slats, and improved armament options. By 1942 all LaGG fighters had internally balanced rudder, retractable tailwheel and wing fuel system for two 22gal drop tanks. Further development led to the switch to an air-cooled radial, from which stemmed all Lavochkin's later piston-engined fighters.

Right: Under test in Japanese hands at Harbin (now Shenyang), this LaGG-3 was flown to a ploughed field in Manchuria by a Russian deserter in 1942. The Japanese were most unimpressed.

Below: This aircraft was built at Plant 153 at Novosibisk, and the non-standard black/green camouflage was paint left over from the tractors previously built there! This aircraft served in the summer of 1942 with the 6th Fighter Aviation Division in the Moscow Corps Command of the IA-PVO.

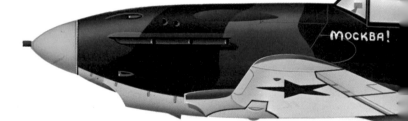

Below: Another LaGG of the 6th Fighter Aviation Division, in this case portrayed in winter camouflage in 1942-3. This was the aircraft of one of the few really successful LaGG-3 pilots, Capt (Col) Gerasim A. Gregoryev, who at this time had 15 confirmed victories. He must have been both skilled and lucky.

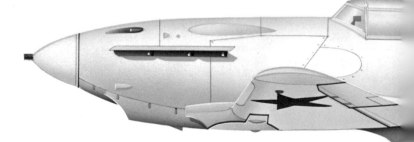

73

Mikoyan MiG-3
MiG-1 (I-61), MiG-3, MiG-5 and MiG-7

Origin: The design bureau of Mikoyan and Gurevich.
Type: Single-seat fighter.
Engine: (-1) one 1,200hp Mikulin AM-35 vee-12 liquid-cooled; (-3) one 1,350hp AM-35A; (-5) one 1,600hp ASh-82A 14-cylinder radial; (-7) one 1,700hp VK-107A vee-12.
Dimensions: Span (all) 33ft 9½in (10·3m); length (-1, -3) 26ft 9in (8·15m); (-5) about 26ft; (-7) not known; height (-1, -3) reported as 8ft 7in (2·61m).
Weights: Empty (-1) 5,721lb (2595kg); (others) not known; maximum loaded (-1) given as 6,770lb and as 7,290lb; (-3) given as 7,390lb and 7,695lb (3490kg); (-5) normal loaded 7,055lb (3200kg); (-7) not known.
Performance: Maximum speed (-1) 390mph (628km/h); (-3) 398mph (640km/h), (also given as 407mph); (-5) over 400mph; (-7) probably over 440mph; initial climb (-1) 3,280ft (1000m)/min; (-3) 3,937ft (1200m)/min; (-5, -7) not known; service ceiling (-1, -3) 39,370ft (12,000m); (-5) not known; (-7) 42,650ft (13,000m); range (-1) 454 miles (730km); (-3) 776 miles (1250km); (-5, -7) not known.
Armament: (-1, -3) one 12·7mm BS and two 7·62mm ShKAS all in nose, later supplemented as field modification by underwing pods for two further unsynchronised BS; underwing rails for six RS-82 rockets or two bombs up to 220lb (100kg) each or two chemical containers; (-5) as above except four 7·62mm ShKAS disposed around cowling, no BS guns; (-7) not known but probably included 20mm ShVAK firing through propeller hub.
History: First flight (I—61) 5 April (also reported as March) 1940; (production MiG-1) September 1940; (MiG-3) about May 1941; final delivery (MiG-3) late 1941; first flight (-5) 1942; (MiG-7) 1943.
User: Soviet Union.

Below: Seen in summer camouflage, this MiG-3 served in 1942 with an unknown IAP (fighter regiment), probably in the reconnaissance role.

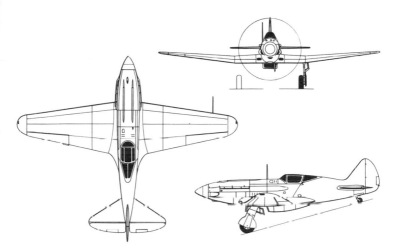

Above: Most MiG-3s had a cockpit canopy and radio mast.

Development: There were probably several new Soviet fighter prototypes in 1938–40, but apart from the Yak-1 information is available on only one other, the I-61 designed by the new partnership of Artem I. Mikoyan and Mikhail I. Gurevich. Though handicapped by its long and heavy engine, which held the armament to a poor level, the mixed wood/metal fighter was a fair performer and went into production as the MiG-1, its only serious vice being an extreme tendency to swing on take-off and landing. In view of the amazing rapidity of its development this was an acceptable penalty and 2,100 are said to have been delivered before it was replaced in production by the refined MiG-3 with more powerful engine, new propeller, additional ▶

Left: One of the few early MiGs to be familiar outside the Soviet Union from wartime photographs, this winter-painted example served in December 1941 with No 34 IAP based at Vnukovo, today one of Moscow's airports and at that time location of the MiG production factory, Zavod 1. IAP 34 was part of the Moscow Western Sector of the IA-PVO, fighter-aviation air defence of the homeland. The inscription meant "For the Fatherland".

fuel tank, increased dihedral and sliding canopy. "Several thousand" are said to have been delivered, but despite adding extra guns they were no match for Luftwaffe fighters and by 1942 were being used for armed reconnaissance and close support. The MiG-5 was used in only small numbers, and few details are available of the all-metal high-altitude MiG-7 with pressurised cockpit.

Below: A winter-painted MiG-3 also seen in the foreground of the photograph, which was taken in early 1942 when the operating unit, 12 IAP, converted from the Yak-1 and was awarded the coveted "Guards" title. Based in Moscow Military District, this unit had wings painted red on the upper surfaces to assist rescue in winter.

Polikarpov I-15 and 153

TsKB-3, I-15, I-15bis, I-153

Origin: The design bureau of Nikolai N. Polikarpov.
Type: Single-seat fighter (15bis, 153, fighter-bomber).
Engine: (15) one 700hp Shvetsov M-25 (Wright Cyclone); (15bis) 750hp M-25B; (153) 1,000hp M-63, all nine-cylinder radials.
Dimensions: Span 29ft 11½in (9·13m); (bis) 33ft 6in; (153) 32ft 9¾in; length 20ft 7½in (6·29m); (bis) 20ft 9¼in; (153) 20ft 3in; height 9ft 7in (2·92m); (bis) 9ft 10in; (153) 9ft 3in.
Weights: Empty 2,597lb (1178kg); (bis) 2,880lb; (153) 3,168lb; maximum loaded 3,027–3,135lb (1370–1422kg); (bis) 4,189lb; (153) 4,431lb.
Performance: Maximum speed 224mph (360km/h); (bis) 230mph; (153) 267mph; initial climb (all) about 2,500ft (765m)/min; service ceiling 32,800ft (10,000m); (bis) 26,245ft; (153) 35,100ft; range 450 miles (720km); (bis) 280 miles; (153) 298 miles.
Armament: Four (sometimes two) 7·62mm DA or ShKAS in fuselage; (bis) as 15, plus two 110lb (50kg) or four 55lb bombs or six RS-82 rockets; (153) as 15bis but two 165lb bombs.
History: First flight (TsKB-3) October 1933; service delivery 1934; service delivery (bis) 1937; (153) 1939.
Users: China, Finland (captured Soviet), Soviet Union, Spain (Republican).

Development: One might jump to the conclusion that these Polikarpov biplanes were superseded by the I-16 monoplane (p. 186). In fact the I-16 flew before any of them, was in service first and, in 1939, was replaced in Mongolia by the more agile I-153! Polikarpov's bureau began work on the TsKB-3 in 1932, when the earlier I-5 was in full production. Unlike the I-5 the new fighter had a small lower wing and large upper gull wing curved down at the roots to meet the fuselage. As the I-15 the highly manoeuvrable fighter gained a world altitude record before serving in very large numbers (about 550) in Spain, where it was dubbed "Chato" (flat-nosed). It even served against the Finns and Luftwaffe, but by 1937 was being replaced by the I-15bis with continuous upper wing carried on struts. Over 300 of these served in Spain, and many were used as dive bombers against the Germans in 1941. The ultimate development was the powerful 153, with retractable landing gear, either wheels or skis folding to the rear. Some

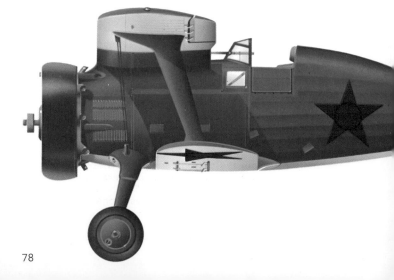

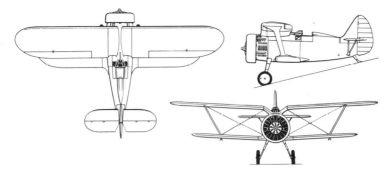

Above: Polikarpov I-15, with guns shown as white dots in front view.

thousands served in the Far East, Spain, Finland and on the Eastern Front. Later sub-types had variable-pitch propellers and drop tanks well outboard under the lower wings. *continued* ▶

Above: The Luftwaffe estimated the VVS (Red Air Forces) lost 2,200 I-15, 15bis and 153 type fighters in the first week of the German invasion in June 1941. Luftwaffe intelligence officers paid attention to all wrecks discovered. This almost undamaged I-153 has eight RS-82 rocket rails under the outer wings. Extremely agile, the 153 was produced after 1939 at a higher rate than the monoplane I-16.

Left: An I-15 in typical VVS summer livery of the mid-1930s, at which time it was not uncommon for a black circle to be inscribed within the national insignia. Almost all I-15s had light bomb carriers under the lower wings, though RS-82 rocket rails were seen mainly on the later versions. Points of interest include multiple exhaust stubs, Aldis gunsight and small windows on each side at the front of the cockpit.

Right: Even more bizarre than a biplane fighter in production in World War II with retractable landing gear is a fighter of such form with jet propulsion! Ivan Merkulov was one of the Russian pioneers of simple ramjet engines, and this I-153 was one of at least two Polikarpov biplane fighters (the other being an I-152 or I-15bis in early 1940) used as a testbed. In this aircraft the units were designated DM-4, DM standing for "auxiliary motor"; the ramjets were intended simply to boost the speed of fighters for brief periods. In October 1940 this I-153 was measured at 273 mph (440 km/h) at 6,560 ft (2,000 m), compared with a maximum at this height on piston engine alone of 241 mph (388 km/h).

Below: Even in peacetime Soviet fighters had lived rough, seldom having the luxury of a permanent airfield or hangar. This I-153 was photographed in 1942. Note the Hucks engine-start truck.

Polikarpov I-16

I-16 Types 1, 4, 5, 10, 17, 18, 24, SPB and UTI

Origin: The design bureau of Nikolai N. Polikarpov.
Type: Single-seat fighter (except SPB dive bomber and UTI two-seat trainer).
Engine: (Type 1) one 480hp M-22 (modified Bristol Jupiter) nine-cylinder radial; (Type 4) 725hp M-25A (modified Wright Cyclone) of same layout; (Types 5, 10, 17) 775hp M-25B; (Types 18 and 24) 1,000hp Shvetsov M-62R (derived from M-25).
Dimensions: Span 29ft 6½in (9·00m); length (to Type 17) 19ft 11in (6·075 m); (18, 24 and UTI) 20ft 1¼in (6·125m); height (to 17) 8ft 1¼in (2·45m); (18, 24) 8ft 5in (2·56m).
Weights: Empty (1) 2,200lb (998kg); (4, 5, 10) 2,791lb (1266kg); (18) 3,110lb (1410kg); (24) 3,285lb (1490kg); loaded (1) 2,965lb (1345kg); (4) 3,135lb (1422kg); (5) 3,660lb (1660kg); (10) 3,782lb (1715kg); (17) 3,990lb (1810kg); (18) 4,034lb (1830kg); (24) 4,215lb (1912kg) (24 overload, 4,546lb, 2062kg).

Below: This Type 24 served on the Central Sector in 1941. Slogan is "For Stalin!"

It was service for Republican Spain that brought the I-16 to the notice of the outside world. This type 10 is seen in Nationalist markings after the Republican defeat in 1939.

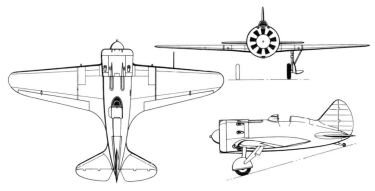

Above: An I-16 Type 24; the ailerons also formed split flaps.

Performance: Maximum speed (1) 224mph (360km/h); (4–18) 280–288 mph (450–465km/h); (24) 326mph (525km/h); initial climb (4–24, typical) 2,790ft (850m)/min; service ceiling (typical) 29,500ft (9000m); range (1–18) 500 miles (800km); (24) 248 miles (400km), (with two 22gal drop tanks, 435 miles, 700km).

continued ▶

Below: Many I-16s served with the Chinese; This Type 10 was with the 4th Wing, Chiangkiakow.

Above: A pair of late (M-62 engined) I-16 fighters recorded in a propaganda film made on the Eastern Front in autumn 1941.

5 - 2

Armament: (1, 4, 5) two 7·62mm ShKAS machine guns in wings; (10) two ShKAS in wings, two in top decking of fuselage; (17) two ShKAS in top decking, two 20mm ShVAK cannon in wings; (18) as 10 or 17; (24) as 17; SPB, various guns plus external bomb load of 220lb (100kg). Many versions were later fitted with underwing rails for two RS-82 rockets.

History: First flight (I-16-1) 31 December 1933; production delivery (1) autumn 1934; (4) autumn 1935; final delivery (24) probably early 1942.

Users: China, Soviet Union, Spain (Republican).

Development: Possibly influenced by the Gee Bee racers of the United States, the TsKB-12, or I-16, was an extremely short and simple little fighter which — perhaps because of its slightly "homebuilt" appearance — was almost ignored by the West. Nobody outside the Soviet Union appeared to notice that this odd fighter, with wooden monocoque body and metal/fabric wing, was a cantilever monoplane with retractable landing gear and v-p propeller which in its first mass-produced form was 60 75mph faster than contemporary fighters of other countries. It suddenly came into prominence when 475 were shipped to the Spanish Republicans, where its reliability, 1,800 rounds/min guns, manoeuvrability and fast climb and dive surprised its opponents, who called it the "Rata" (rat). A few old Type 10 remained in Spanish use until 1952. Hundreds of several types fought Japanese aircraft over China and Manchuria, where many I-16s were fitted with the new RS-82 rocket. The final, more powerful versions were built in far greater numbers than any others, about one in 30 being a UTI trainer with tandem open cockpits (and in some versions with fixed landing gear). Total production of this extremely important fighter is estimated at 7,000, of which probably 4,000 were engaged in combat duty against the German invader in 1941–43. Heroically flown against aircraft of much later design and often used for deliberate ramming attacks, the stumpy I-16 operated on wheels or skis long after it was obsolete yet today is recognised as one of the really significant combat aircraft of history.

Left: This early (Type 6) I-16 was operational with the 4a Escuadrilla, Grupo núm 31, of the Spanish Republican air force in 1936. Dubbed Mosca by its users, it became better known by the name given it by its Nationalist foes, Rata (rat).

Below: An I-16 Type 24 with skis, though still in dark summer camouflage. This landing gear retracted, but some ski arrangements were fixed.

Yakovlev Yak-1

Ya-26, I-26, Yak-1, Yak-7

Origin: The design bureau of A. S. Yakovlev.
Type: Single-seat fighter.
Engine: Initially, one 1,100hp VK-105PA (M-105PA) vee-12 liquid-cooled, derived from Hispano-Suiza 12Y; later, 1,260hp VK-105PF.
Dimensions: Span 32ft 9¾in (10m); length 27ft 9¾in (8·48m); height 8ft 8in (2·64m).
Weights: Empty (early I-26) 5,137lb (2375kg); maximum loaded 6,217lb (2890kg).
Performance: Maximum speed 373mph (600km/h), 310mph (500km/h) at sea level; initial climb 3,940ft (1200m)/min; service ceiling 32,800ft (10,000m); range, 582 miles (850km).
Armament: (I-26) one 20mm ShVAK cannon, with 120 rounds, firing through propeller hub and two 7·62mm ShKAS machine guns, each with 375 rounds, above engine. (Yak-1, late 1941) one 20mm ShVAK, with 140 rounds, one or two 12·7mm Beresin BS above engine, each with about 348 rounds, and underwing rails for six 25lb (12kg) RS-82 rockets. Some, wing racks for two 110lb or 220lb (50 or 100kg) bombs.
History: First flight March 1939; service delivery (pre-production) October 1940; (production) July 1941.
User: Soviet Union.

continued ▶

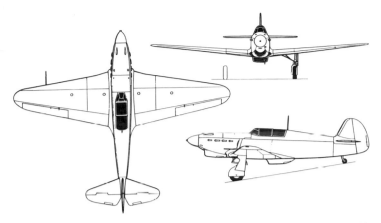

Above: A standard Yak-1, similar in general outline to the Yak-7A.

Left: Seen in winter camouflage, this Yak-1 operated on the Central Sector in January 1942. Note the different type of rear-view windows (instead of a completely transparent rear decking) and absence of a radio mast. The different rear windows appeared after the evacuation of production to Kamensk-Uralsk in late 1941 and is seen on about one-quarter of Yak-1s.

Below: Thousands of women flew combat aircraft in the Soviet Union in World War II, the top-scorer being Lt Lily Litvyak of No 73 IAP (third from left).

Development: In 1939 the Soviet government announced specifications for a new fighter. Surprisingly, the best of four rival prototypes was that from young Alexander S. Yakovlev, who had previously designed only gliders and sporting machines. His Ya-26 earned him fame and riches, and in June 1941 was cleared for production as the chief Soviet fighter. At this time the designation was changed from I-26 to Yak-1, in conformity with the new policy of designation by design bureau rather than by function. In the same month the German hordes swept in from the West and the entire production line was moved 1,000 miles eastwards to Kamensk-Uralsk.

Below: Yak-1, with the inscription "Death to Fascists" near the 27 victory stars, as flown in 1942 by Lt M. D. Baranov of 183 Fighter Regiment.

Despite this there was a delay of only about six weeks, and about 500 Yak-1 were in action by the end of 1941. With a wooden wing and steel-tube body it was a solid and easily maintained machine, with excellent handling. In parallel came the UTI-26 trainer, with tandem seats, which went into production as the Yak-7V. In late 1941 this was modified with lower rear fuselage to improve view and this in turn led to the Yak-7B fighter which in early 1942 supplanted the Yak-1 in production. Such was the start of the second-biggest aircraft-production programme in history, which by 1945 had delivered 37,000 fighters.

Bottom: A Yak-7A fresh off the line at Kamensk-Uralsk, probably in August 1942.

Yakovlev Yak-3

Yak-1M and -3

Origin: The design bureau of A. S. Yakovlev.
Type: Single-seat fighter.
Engine: (-1M) one 1,260hp Klimov VK-105PF vee-12 liquid-cooled; (-3) 1,225hp VK-105PF-2; (final series) 1,650hp VK-107A.
Dimensions: Span 30ft 2¼in (9·20m); length 27ft 10¼in (8·50m); height 7ft 10in (2·39m).
Weights: Empty (VK-105) 4,960lb (2250kg); maximum loaded 5,864lb (2660kg).
Performance: Maximum speed (VK-105) 404mph (650km/h); (VK-107) 447mph (720km/h); initial climb (105) 4,265ft (1300m)/min; (107) 5,250ft (1600m)/min; service ceiling (105) 35,450ft (10,800m); range (105) 506 miles (815km).
Armament: One 20mm ShVAK, with 120 rounds, and two 12·7mm BS, each with 250 rounds.
History: First flight (-1M) 1942; (-3) spring 1943; service delivery (-3) about July 1943; (-3 with VK-107) not later than January 1944.
Users: Czech, French and Polish units, and Soviet Union.

Development: As early as 1941 Yakovlev was considering means whereby he could wring the highest possible performance out of the basic Yak-1 design. As there was no immediate prospect of more power, and armament and equipment were already minimal, the only solution seemed to be to cut down the airframe, reduce weight and reduce drag. In the Yak-1M the wing was reduced in size, the oil cooler replaced by twin small coolers in the wing roots, the rear fuselage cut down and a simple clear-view canopy fitted, the coolant radiator duct redesigned and other detail changes made. The result was a fighter even more formidable in close combat than the -1 and -9 families, though it landed faster. The production -3 was further refined by a thick coat of hard-wearing wax polish, and after meeting the new fighter during the mighty Kursk battle in the summer of 1943 the Luftwaffe recognised it had met its match. Indeed by 1944 a general directive had gone out to Luftwaffe units on the Eastern Front to "avoid combat below 5000m with Yakovlev fighters lacking an oil cooler under the nose"! To show what the Yak-3 could do when bravely handled, despite its ▶

Right: Derived from the Yak-1M (which, except for a single example, had the original size of wing) the Yak-3 was a nimble dogfighter with a smaller wing and other changes to reduce drag, including wing-root oil coolers and a long radiator duct.

Below: Yak-3 as flown by Maj Gen Zakharov, CO of the 303 Fighter Aviation Division, 1944, sporting the Order of the Red Banner (Military) emblem on the engine cowling and his personal emblem under the cockpit.

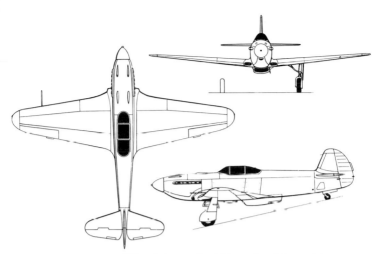

Above: Three-view of Yak-3 (some had hinged rudder-tab).

Above: Yak-3s of an unidentified IAP probably in the summer or autumn of 1944. Apart from the small wing and clean lower cowl the Yak-3 could be identified by the two-piece landing-gear fairings, which were not seen on other Yaks since the Yak-1.

armament — which was trivial compared with that of the German fighters — on 14 July 1944 a force of 18 met 30 Luftwaffe fighters and destroyed 15 for the loss of one Yak-3. Small wonder that, offered all available Soviet, British or American fighters, the Normandie-Niemen Group changed from the Yak-9 to the Yak-3 and scored the last 99 of their 273 victories on these machines. It was natural that the more powerful VK-107 engine should have been fitted to the Yak-3, though the designation was not changed. After prolonged trials in early 1944 the Soviet test centre judged the 107-engined aircraft to be 60–70mph faster than either a Bf 109G or an Fw 190, but the re-engined aircraft was just too late to see action in World War II. As in the case of the Yak-1 and -9, there were various experimental conversions of the Yak-3, the best-known being the mixed-power Yak-3 ZhRD of early 1945, which reached at least 485mph (780km/h) on a VK-105 and a liquid-propellant rocket. A more radical installation was the Yak-7VRD with two large ramjets under the wings. Total production of the Yak-1, -3, -7 and -9 was not less than 37,000. These fighters may have been smaller and simpler than those of other nations in World War II but they served the Soviet Union well in its hour of great need. They conserved precious material, kept going under almost impossible airfield and maintenance conditions and consistently out-performed their enemies.

Below: One of the first production Yak-3s, which gave the Axis
fighter pilots on the Eastern Front an unpleasant shock around
May 1944. Later its performance was further enhanced by fitting
the VK-107 engine; this variant, the Yak-3U, was all-metal.

Yakovlev Yak-9

Yak-9, -9D, -9T, -9U and -9P

Origin: The design bureau of A. S. Yakovlev.
Type: Single-seat fighter (some, fighter-bomber).
Engine: (-9, D and T) one 1,260hp Klimov VK-105PF vee-12 liquid-cooled; (U, P) one 1,650hp VK-107A.
Dimensions: Span 32ft 9¾in (10m); length (-9, D, T) 28ft 0½in (8·54m); (U, P) 28ft 6½in (8·70m); height 8ft (2·44m).
Weights: Empty (T) 6,063lb (2750kg); (U) 5,100lb (2313kg); maximum loaded (T) 7,055lb (3200kg); (U) 6,988lb (3170kg).
Performance: Maximum speed (9) 373mph (600km/h); (D) 359mph (573km/h); (T) 367mph (590km/h); (U) 435mph (700km/h); (P) 416mph (670km/h); initial climb (typical, 9, D, T) 3,795ft (1150m)/min; (U, P) 4,920ft (1500m)/min; service ceiling (all) about 34,500ft (10,500m); range (most) 520–550 miles (840–890km); (D) 840 miles (1350km); (DD) 1,367 miles (2200km).
Armament: (Most) one 20mm ShVAK, with 100 rounds, and two 12·7mm BS, each with 250 rounds, plus two 220lb (100kg) bombs; (B) internal bay for 880lb (400kg) bomb load; (T) gun through propeller changed to 37mm NS-P37 with 32 rounds; (K) this changed for 45mm cannon; certain aircraft had 12·7mm BS firing through hub.
History: First flight (7DI) June 1942; (9M) about August 1942; (D, T) probably late 1943; (U) January 1944; (P) August 1945; final delivery (P) about 1946.
Users: (Wartime) France, Poland, Soviet Union.

Development: The Yak-7DI introduced light-alloy wing spars and evolved into the Yak-9, most-produced Soviet aircraft apart from the Il-2. Able to outfly the Bf 109G, which it met over Stalingrad in late 1942, the -9 was developed into the anti-tank -9T, bomber -9B, long-range -9D and very long-range -9DD. The DD escorted US heavy bombers, and once a large group flew from the Ukraine to Bari (southern Italy) to help Jugoslav partisans. The famed Free French Normandie-Niemen Group and both free Polish squadrons used various first-generation -9s. With a complete switch

Below: French Normandie-Niemen regiment Yak-9.

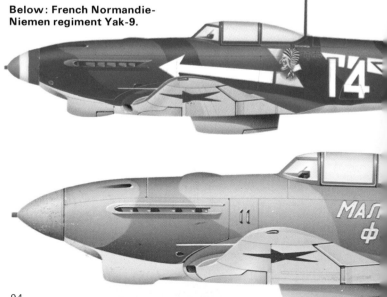

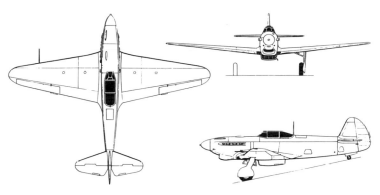

Above: Standard Yak-9; long-range -9D and -9DD externally similar.

to stressed-skin structure and the VK-107 engine there was a dramatic jump in performance, the -9U entering service in the second half of 1944 and flying rings round the 109 and 190. The U could be identified by the smooth cowl, the oil coolers being in the wing root; the post war -9P, encountered in Korea, had a DF loop under a transparent cover in the rear fuselage.

Above: Yak-9Ds of a Guards IAP over the Crimea in 1944; nearest the camera the aircraft of Col Avdyeyev (15 victories).

Below: A Yak-7B, derived from Yak-1, but in technology and appearance closer to the Yak-9.

USA

Remote geographically from any evident potential enemies, the mighty USA devoted only modest sums to warplanes until war in China, Spain and then Europe forced the giant to stir in the late 1930s. By this time, despite an industry second to none in its engineering skills, technology and production potential, the nation had slipped markedly in fighter design and had nothing to match the Bf 109E or Spitfire. This is the more remarkable when it is realized that Americans led the world in stressed-skin structures, variable-pitch propellers, flaps and pressurization, and had fiercely competing engine builders who before World War II were offering engines of 1,500hp.

One of the classic stories of procurement relates how, in November 1939, North American Aviation was asked by Britain to build the Curtiss P-40 for the RAF. "Dutch" Kindelberger, the company's president, replied NAA could design a much better fighter from scratch. The P-40, though mediocre, was a known quantity, whereas NAA had no experience with fighters. The British wasted six months before finally giving their consent; even then they did nothing to ensure the resulting NA-73 had a Merlin engine. Named Mustang, the NA-73 was a masterpiece, with superior speed, superb handling and three times the range of a Spitfire. Later, with a two-stage Packard Merlin, it mastered the Luftwaffe even over distant Berlin.

One of the best Allied fighters, the Merlin-Mustang, did not see action until 1944, yet accounted for almost 14,000 of the 15,586 Mustangs built. This P-51B was flown by ace Don Gentile.

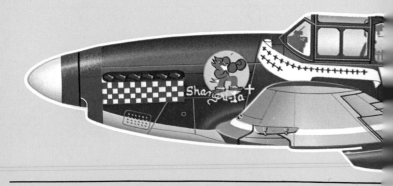

The unorthodox P-38 was a fine long-range fighter and good bomber, but with a 52-foot wingspan it rolled too slowly for dogfighting. The mighty P-47 was possibly the war's greatest ground-attack aircraft, but the mass-produced P-39 and P-40 were also-rans used mainly and successfully as fighter-bombers.

One area where the United States excelled was in naval aircraft. Though the Brewster F2A is best forgotten, its rival, the Grumman F4F, held the fort over Allied oceans almost single-handed until in 1943 the formidable F6F and F4U (and the British Seafire) made their presence felt. Thanks to Pratt & Whitney's R-2800, a sheer package of power, the F6F and F4U could move their ponderous bulk better than their smaller and much lighter enemies. The F6F was more numerous among Pacific fighter squadrons, and did far more than any other aircraft to destroy Japan's command of the air. But the bent-wing F4U, at first judged tricky and unfit for carrier operation (a belief disproved by the British Fleet Air Arm even with baby carriers), was finally recognised as possibly the greatest fighter of the entire war. It outflew such doughty opponents as the P-47M, P-51H and Japan's Ki-84!

America built a wealth of fighter prototypes during the war, some of them bizarre in design. That none saw production is testimony to such machines as the P-51 and F4U, two of the most successful fighters in history.

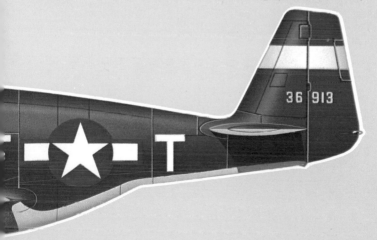

Bell P-39 Airacobra

P-39 to P39Q Airacobra (data for P-39L)

Origin: Bell Aircraft Corporation.
Type: Single-seat fighter.
Engine: 1,325hp Allison V-1710-63 vee-12 liquid-cooled.
Dimensions: Span 34ft 0in (10·37m); length 30ft 2in (9·2m); height (one prop-blade vertical) 11ft 10in (3·63m).
Weights: Empty 5,600lb (2540kg); loaded 7,780lb (3530kg).
Performance: Maximum speed 380mph (612km/h); initial climb 4,000ft (1220m)/min; service ceiling 35,000ft (10,670m); ferry range with drop tank at 160mph (256km/h) 1,475 miles (2360km).
Armament: One 37mm cannon with 30 rounds (twice as many as in first sub-types), two synchronised 0·5in Colt-Brownings and two or four 0·30in in outer wings.
History: First flight of XP-39 April 1939: (P-39F to M sub-types, 1942); final batch (P-39Q) May 1944.
Users: France, Italy (CB), Portugal, Soviet Union, UK (RAF, briefly), US (AAF).

Development: First flown as a company prototype in 1939, this design by R. J. Woods and O. L. Woodson was unique in having a nosewheel-type landing gear and the engine behind the pilot. The propeller was driven by a long shaft under the pilot's seat and a reduction gearbox in the nose, the latter also containing a big 37mm cannon firing through the propeller hub. Other guns were also fitted in the nose, the first production aircraft, the P-39C of 1941, having two 0·30in and two 0·5in all synchronised to fire past the propeller. Britain ordered the unconventional fighter in 1940 and in June 1941 the first Airacobra I arrived, with the 37mm gun and 15 rounds having been replaced by a 20mm Hispano with 60. Two 0·303in Brownings in the nose and four more in the wings completed the armament. No 601 Sqn did poorly with it and failed to keep the unusual aircraft serviceable, but the US Army Air Force used it in big numbers. Altogether 9,588 were built and used with fair success in the Mediterranean and Far East, some 5,000 being supplied to the Soviet Union, mainly through Iran. Biggest production version was the P-39Q, of which over 4,900 were built. The P-39 was succeeded in production in 1944 by the P-63 Kingcobra.

continued ▶

Below: This P-39L, an interim model with Curtiss propeller, flew with the 91st FS, 81st FG.

Right: Disproving the wartime joke about the "P-400 — a P-40 with a Zero in its tail", this really was designated P-400. These were ex-RAF aircraft with 20mm Hispano still fitted and British serial unerased.

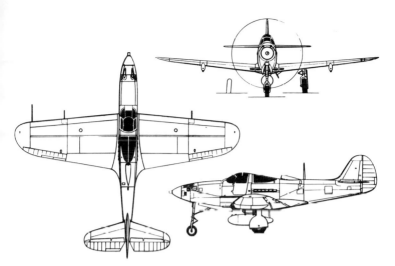

Above: Bell P-39Q, the most numerous model, with drop tank.

Above: Many Allied nations used Airacobras, notably the Soviet Union which liked the US fighter for its ground-attack capability. This example, a P-39N, is shown operating with the Italian Co-Belligerent AF, which was busy in Balkan airspace in 1944.

Part of a US Army Air Corps formation of P-39D Airacobras, probably in 1942. This model saw action in the Pacific in the course of that year.

Another 1942 photograph, showing one of the first P-39Ds, the first model judged combat-ready. Note the masking tape round the radio door, and the red star-centres painted over to avoid confusion with the Japanese Hinomaru.

Bell P-59 Airacomet
YP-59, P-59A and XF2L-1

Origin: Bell Aircraft Corporation.
Type: Single-seat jet fighter trainer.
Engines: Two 2,000lb (907kg) thrust General Electric J31-GE-3 turbojets.
Dimensions: Span 45ft 6in (13·87m); length 38ft 1½in (11·63m); height 12ft 0in (3·66m).
Weights: Empty 7,950lb (3610kg); loaded 12,700lb (5760kg).
Performance: Maximum speed 413mph (671km/h); service ceiling 46,200ft (14,080m); maximum range with two 125 Imp gal drop tanks 520 miles (837km) at 289mph (465km/h) at 20,000ft (6096m).
Armament: Usually none, but some YP-59 fitted with nose guns (eg one 37mm cannon and three 0·5in) and one rack under each wing for bomb as alternative to drop tank.
History: First flight (XP-59A) 1 October 1942; (production P-59A) 7 August 1944.
Users: US (AAF, Navy); (one UK in exchange for Meteor I).

Development: In June 1941 the US government and General ''Hap'' Arnold of the Army Air Corps were told of Britain's development of the turbojet engine. On 5 September 1941 Bell Aircraft was requested to design a jet fighter and in the following month a Whittle turbojet, complete engineering drawings and a team from Power Jets Ltd arrived from Britain to hasten proceedings. The result was that Bell flew the first American jet in one year from the start of work. The Whittle-type centrifugal engines, Americanised

Below: The 16th P-59A, without armament fitted and bearing the red-outlined national marking of 1942—43. Pleasant to fly, the basic type was simply too big for the low thrust engines, and was inferior in performance to a P-51.

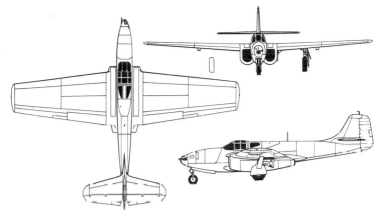

Above: Bell P-59A with broader but cut-down vertical tail.

and made by General Electric as the 1,100lb (500kg) thrust 1-A, were installed under the wing roots, close to the centreline and easily accessible (two were needed to fly an aircraft of useful size). Flight development went extremely smoothly, and 12 YP-59As for service trials were delivered in 1944. Total procurement amounted to 66 only, including three XF2L-1s for the US Navy, and the P-59A was classed as a fighter-trainer because it was clear it would not make an effective front-line fighter. But in comparison with the fast timescale it was a remarkable achievement, performance being very similar to that attained with the early Meteors.

Below left: Devoid of any tail number, this is one of the original three XP-59 prototypes, pictured at Lake Muroc. The designation P-59 had previously been that of a Bell piston-engined fighter, and as a security cover the first XP-59 was fitted with a dummy propeller.

Below: Another view of an early Airacomet, in this case a YP-59, seen being towed across the apron.

Bell P-63 Kingcobra

P-63A to E and RP-63

Origin: Bell Aircraft Corporation, Buffalo, NY.

Type: Single-seat fighter-bomber.

Engine: One Allison V-1710 vee-12 liquid-cooled, (A) 1,500hp (war emergency rating) V-1710-93, (C) 1,800hp V-1710-117.

Dimensions: Span 38ft 4in (11·68m); length 32ft 8in (9·96m); height 12ft 7in (3·84m).

Weights: Empty (A) 6,375lb (2892kg); maximum (A) 10,500lb (4763kg).

Performance: Maximum speed (all) 410mph (660km/h); typical range with three bombs 340 miles (547km); ferry range with three tanks 2,575 miles (4143km).

Armament: Usually one 37mm and four 0·5in, plus up to three 500lb (227kg) bombs.

History: First flight 7 December 1942; service delivery October 1943; final delivery early 1945.

Users: Brazil, France, Italy, Soviet Union, US (AAF).

continued ▶

Almost three-quarters of the 3,303 Kingcobras went to the Soviet Union. This photograph, taken in late 1943, shows P-63As awaiting collection at the Buffalo plant.

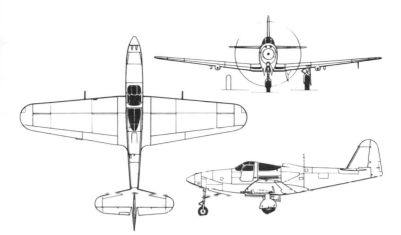

Above: Bell P-63A with outboard bomb racks and radio mast.

Development: Though it looked like a P-39 with a different tail, in fact the P-63 was a completely different design, greatly improved in the light of painful combat experience. It fully met a February 1941 Army requirement, but air war developed so fast that — though Bell did a competent job to a fast schedule — the P-63 was outclassed before it reached the squadrons. It never fought with the US forces, but 2,421 of the 3,303 built went to the Soviet Union where their tough airframes and good close-support capability made them popular. At least 300 went to the Free French, in both A and C variants (both of which had a wealth of sub-types). The D had a sliding bubble canopy and larger wing, and the E extra fuel. The only USAAF Kingcobras were 332 completed or modified as heavily armoured RP-63A or C manned target aircraft, shot at by live "frangible" (easily shattered) bullets. Each hit made a powerful lamp light at the tip of the spinner.

Left and below: Two aircraft from the same late production block of P-63As (delivered unpainted), with outboard wing racks, four-blade Aeroproducts propeller and radio mast. Armament comprises a 37mm gun (in this model the M10, which did not project externally, with ammunition magazine enlarged from 30 to 58 rounds) and four 0.5in.

Brewster F2A Buffalo

F2A-1 (239), F2A-2 (339), F2A-3 and 439 Buffalo 1 (data for F2A-2)

Origin: Brewster Aircraft Company, Long Island City.
Type: Single-seat carrier or land-based fighter.
Engine: 1,100hp Wright R-1820-40 (G-205A) Cyclone nine-cylinder radial.
Dimensions: Span 35ft (10·67m); length 26ft 4in (8m); height 12ft 1in (3·7m).
Weights: Empty 4,630lb (2100kg); loaded 7,055lb (3200kg) (varied from 6,848–7,159lb).
Performance: Maximum speed 300mph (483km/h); initial climb 3,070ft (935m)/min; service ceiling 30,500ft (9300m); range 650–950 miles (1045–1530km).
Armament: Four machine guns, two in fuselage and two in wing, calibre of each pair being 0·30in, 0·303in or, mostly commonly, 0·50in.
History: First flight (XF2A-1) January 1938; first service delivery April 1939; termination of production 1942.
Users: Australia, Finland, Netherlands (E. Indies), New Zealand, UK (RAF), US (Navy, Marines).

Development: The Brewster company was established in 1810 to build carriages. In 1935 it plunged into planemaking and secured an order for a US Navy scout-bomber. It also entered a competition for a carrier-based monoplane fighter and won. Not surprisingly, it took almost two years — a long time in those days — to fly the first prototype. Yet one must give the team their due, for the F2A-1 was confirmed as the Navy's choice for its first monoplane fighter even after Grumman had flown the G.36 (Wildcat). In June 1938 a contract was placed for 54 of these tubby mid-wingers, then armed with one 0·50in and one 0·30in machine guns. Only 11 reached USS *Saratoga*; the rest went to Finland, where from February 1940 until the end of World War II they did extremely well. The US Navy bought 43 more powerful and more heavily armed F2A-2 (Model 339), and then 108 F2A-3 with armour and self-sealing tanks. Of these, 21 in the hands of the Marine Corps put up a heroic struggle in the first Battle of Midway. In 1939 bulk orders were placed by Belgium and Britain, and the RAF operated 170 delivered in 1941 to Singapore. Another 72 were bought by the Netherlands.

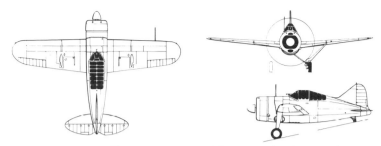

Above: Brewster F2A-3, the final US Navy production version.

Above: The wartime censor has obliterated the RAF code letters on this Buffalo squadron pictured over Malaya in 1941 in company with a Blenheim IV. Totally outclassed by the rival A6M Zero, the RAF did its best to increase performance by replacing the 0·5-inch guns by 0·303-inch, reducing ammunition to 350 rounds and fuel to a mere 84 gallons. The Brewster remained inferior.

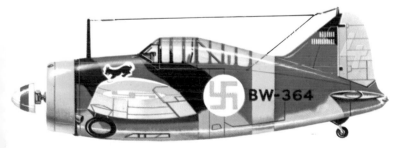

Above: As described in the text, most of the initial production version, the F2A-1, were diverted to Finland, where their robust manoeuvrability made them quite popular. They equipped two squadrons of LeR 2, this particular machine serving with the 3rd Flight of No 24 Squadron based at Römpötissa as late as 1942.

Left: Though it failed to reach customers in Belgium and the Dutch East Indies, the F2A did see action with the British Commonwealth air forces, Fleet Air Arm and (in the F2A-3 form illustrated) with a Marine Corps fighter squadron. The unit was VMF-221, and it suffered heavy casualties at Midway in 1942.

Curtiss Hawk family

A: Hawk 75A, P-36A, Mohawk IV
B: Hawk 81A, P-40C, Tomahawk IIB
C: Hawk 87D, P-40F, Kittyhawk II
D: Hawk 87M, P-40N, Kittyhawk IV

Origin: Curtiss-Wright Corporation.
Type: (A) single-seat fighter, (B) single-seat fighter, reconnaissance and ground attack; (C, D) single-seat fighter bomber.
Engine: (A) P-36A, 1,050hp Pratt & Whitney R-1830-13 Twin Wasp 14-cylinder two-row radial; Hawk 75A and Mohawk, 1,200hp Wright GR-1820-G205A Cyclone nine-cylinder radial; (B) 1,040hp Allison V-1710-33 vee-12 liquid-cooled; (C) 1,300hp Packard V-1650-1 (R-R Merlin) vee-12 liquid-cooled; (D) 1,200hp Allison V-1710-81, -99 or -115 vee-12 liquid-cooled.
Dimensions: Span 37ft 3½in (11·36m); length (A) 28ft 7in (8·7m), (B) 31ft 8½in (9·7m); (C) 31ft 2in (9·55m) or 33ft 4in (10·14m); (D) 33ft 4in (10·14m); height (A) 9ft 6in (2·89m), (B, C, D) 12ft 4in (3·75m).
Weights: Empty (A) 4,541lb (2060kg), (B) 5,812lb (2636kg), (C) 6,550lb (2974kg), (D) 6,700lb (3039kg); loaded (A) 6,662lb (3020kg), (B) 7,459lb (3393kg), (C) 8,720lb (3960kg), (D) 11,400lb (5008kg).
Performance: Maximum speed (A) 303mph (488km/h), (B) 345mph (555km/h), (C) 364mph (582km/h), (D) 343mph (552km/h); initial climb (A) 2,500ft (762m)/min, (B) 2,650ft (807m)/min, (C) 2,400ft (732m)/min, (D) 2,120ft (646m)/min; service ceiling (all) about 30,000ft (9144m); range on internal fuel (A) 680 miles (1,100km), (B) 730 miles (1175km), (C) 610 miles (976km), (D) 750 miles (1207km).
Armament: (A) P-36A, one 0·50in and one 0·30in Brownings above engine; P-36C, as P-36A with two 0·30in in wings; Hawk 75A/Mohawk IV, six 0·303in (four in wings); (B) six 0·303in (four in wings); (C, D) six 0·50in in wings with 281 rounds per gun (early P-40N, only four); bomb load (A) underwing racks for total of 400lb (181kg); (B) nil; (C) one 500lb on centreline and 250lb (113kg) under each wing; (D) 500 or 600lb (272kg) on centreline and 500lb under each wing.
History: First flight (Model 75 prototype) May 1935; (first Y1P-36) January 1937; (first production P-36A) April 1938; (XP-40) October 1938; (P-40) January 1940; (P-40D) 1941; (P-40F) 1941; (P-40N) 1943; final delivery (P-40N-40 and P-40R) December 1944.
Users: Argentina, Australia, Belgium, Bolivia, Brazil, Canada, China, Colombia, Egypt, Finland, France, Iraq, Italy (CB), Netherlands, New Zealand, Norway, Peru, Portugal, S. Africa, Soviet Union, Turkey, UK (RAF), US (AAC/AAF).

Development: In November 1934 Curtiss began the design of a completely new "Hawk" fighter with cantilever monoplane wing, backwards retracting landing gear (the wheels turning 90° to lie inside the wing) and all-metal ▶

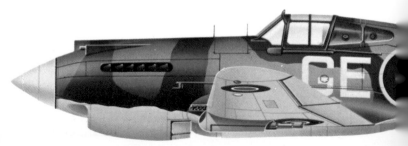

110

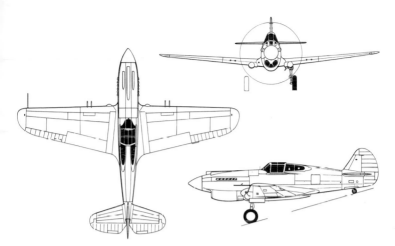

Above: Curtiss P-40C (Hawk 81A and Tomahawk II similar).

Below: Two of the many variants of Hawk 75 that saw action in World War II were the Hawk 75A-7 of the Netherlands East Indies (R-1820 Cyclone) and the Hawk 75-C1 (maker's designation, 75A-1) of the Armée de l'Air (R-1830 Twin Wasp). Other sub-types saw action with the RAF (India), Finland, and USAAF (Hawaii).

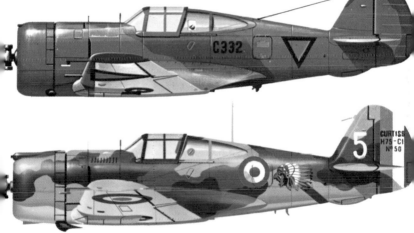

Left: AH972 was a Tomahawk IIA (Hawk 81A-2), one of the first Hawks supplied on UK account instead of being diverted from a French order. Basically similar to the P-40B it had two 0.5in guns on the cowling and two 0.303in in the wings. The much more numerous Tomahawk IIB had an armament of six 0.303in. This machine served with 349 (Belgian) Sqn RAF at Ikeja, Nigeria.

stressed-skin construction. After being tested by the Army Air Corps this design was put into production as the P-36A, marking a major advance in speed though not in firepower. Successive types of P-36 and its export counterpart, the Hawk 75A, had different engines and additional guns and the Hawk 75A was bought in large numbers by many countries and made under licence in several. Biggest customer was the French Armée de l'Air, which began to receive the H75A in March 1939. Five groups — GC I/4, II/4, I/5, II/5 and III/2 — wrote a glorious chapter over France in May 1940, invariably outnumbered and usually outperformed, but destroying 311 of the Luftwaffe, more than the total H75A strength when France fell. The rest of the French orders were supplied to the RAF as Mohawks, serving mainly on the Burma front.

More than 1,300 radial-engined models were delivered, but the real story began with the decision in July 1937 to build the P-40, with the liquid-cooled Allison engine. This was a novel and untried engine in a land where aircraft engines had become universally air-cooled, and teething troubles were long and severe. Eventually, towards the end of 1940, the P-40B and RAF Tomahawk I were cleared for combat duty and the process of development began. The rest of the aircraft was almost unchanged and in comparison with the Bf109 or Spitfire the early P-40 showed up badly, except in the twin attributes of manoeuvrability and strong construction. Eventually the RAF, RAAF and SAAF took 885 of three marks of Tomahawk, used as low-level army co-operation machines in Britain and as ground attack fighters in North Africa. Many hundreds of other P-40Bs and Cs were supplied to the US Army, Soviet Union, China and Turkey.

With the P-40D a new series of Allison engines allowed the nose to be shortened and the radiator was deepened, changing the appearance of the aircraft. The fuselage guns were finally thrown out and the standard armament became the much better one of six "fifties" in the wings. The RAF had ordered 560 of the improved fighters in 1940, and they were called ▶

Above: A fine picture of Kittyhawk IIIs of the Desert Air Force returning with empty bomb racks in Tunisia in early 1943. At advanced airfields it was standard practice for an ''erk'' to ride on a wingtip and guide the pilot past potholes and obstructions.

Below: Field maintenance for a P-40F Warhawk, with Packard Merlin whose carb-air inlet was on the underside, not above.

Kittyhawk I. When the US Army bought it the name Warhawk was given to subsequent P-40 versions. The Merlin engine went into production in the USA in 1941 and gave rise to the P-40F; none of the 1,311 Merlin P-40s reached the RAF, most going to the Soviet Union, US Army and Free French. Most Fs introduced a longer fuselage to improve directional stability. Subsequent models had a dorsal fin as well and reverted to the Allison engine. Great efforts were made to reduce weight and improve performance, because the whole family was fundamentally outclassed by the other front-line fighters on both sides; but, predictably, weight kept rising. It reached its peak in the capable and well-equipped P-40N, of which no fewer than 4,219 were built. Some of the early Ns had all the weight-savings and could reach 378mph (608km/h), but they were exceptions. Altogether deliveries of P-40 versions to the US government amounted to 13,738. Though it was foolhardy to tangle with a crack enemy fighter in close combat the Hawk family were tough, nimble and extremely useful weapons, especially in close support of armies.

Right: A 1942 photograph of a P-40E with the anti-swing dorsal fin of the P-40K. Note armament of six "point-fifties".

Right: This P-40K is one of the later K-10 or -15 production blocks with the fuselage length increased from 31ft 2in to 33ft 4in, as in most of the Merlin-engined P-40Fs. This particular example, seen with very necessary drop tank, was designated Kittyhawk III and operated by the RNZAF on Guadalcanal in the closing months of 1942.

Below: Seen in this case operating with the Army Air Corps 77th Fighter Sqn, 20th Pursuit Group, Hamilton Field, California, in 1941, the P-40C usually had two wing guns.

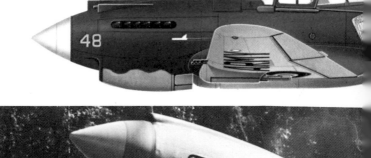

Below: Hawks served in every theatre in World War II, and though inferior as dogfighters against their best enemies they did as much as any other Allied type in the role of tactical fighter-bomber. This USAAF P-40K is about to depart on an interception mission after the alert had sounded at Dobodura, New Guinea, in May 1943. Its unit is the 7th Fighter Group.

Grumman F4F/FM Wildcat
G-36, Martlet, F4F-1 to -4 and
Eastern Aircraft FM-1 and -2

Origin: Grumman Aircraft Engineering Corporation; also built by Eastern Aircraft.

Type: Single-seat naval fighter.

Engine: (XF4F-2) one 1,050hp Pratt & Whitney R-1830-66 Twin Wasp 14-cylinder two-row radial; (G-36A, Martlet I (Wildcat I)) one 1,200hp Wright R-1820-G205A Cyclone nine-cylinder radial; (F4F-3) 1,200hp R-1830-76; (F4F-4 and FM-1 (Wildcat V)) R-1830-86; (FM-2 (Wildcat VI)) 1,350hp R-1820-56.

Dimensions: Span 38ft 0in (11·6m); length 28ft 9in to 28ft 11in (FM-2, 28ft 10in, 8·5m); height 11ft 11in (3·6m).

Weights: Empty (F4F-3) 4,425lb; (F4F-4) 4,649lb; (FM-2) 4,900lb (2226kg); loaded (F4F-3) 5,876lb; (F4F-4) 6,100lb rising to 7,952lb (3607kg) with final FM-1s; (FM-2) 7,412lb.

Performance: Maximum speed (F4F-3) 325mph (523km/h); (F4F-4, FM-1) 318mph (509km/h); (FM-2) 332mph (534km/h); initial climb, typically 2,000ft (610m)/min (3,300ft/min in early versions, 1,920 in main production and over 2,000 for FM-2); service ceiling, typically 35,000ft (10,670m) (more in light early versions); range, typically 900 miles (1448km).

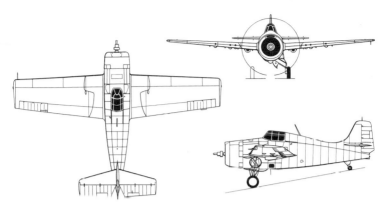

Above: Grumman F4F-4 (FM-1 similar but only four 0·50-in guns).

Armament: (XF4F-2) two 0·5in Colt-Brownings in fuselage; (F4F-3) four 0·5in in outer wings; (F4F-4 and subsequent) six 0·5in in outer wings; (F4F-4, FM-1 and FM-2) underwing racks for two 250lb (113kg) bombs.
History: First flight (XF4F-2) 2 September 1937; (XF4F-3) 12 February 1939; production (G-36 and F4F-3) February 1940; (FM-2) March 1943; final delivery August 1945.
Users: France (FFL), Greece, UK (RN), US (Navy, Marines). *continued* ▶

Left: A US Navy F4F-4 Wildcat in late-war markings (post September 1943 with blue-bordered insignia). This model had a Twin Wasp engine and six guns; this particular aircraft has a vertical radio mast, normally fitted only to the later FM-2.

Below: A Cyclone-powered Martlet IV (later renamed Wildcat IV to fall into line with the name selected by the US Navy) after recovery aboard a Royal Navy Fleet Carrier, probably in 1943. This variant, with four guns, saw much action, particularly with 811 and 882 Sqns.

Development: Designed as a biplane to continue Grumman's very successful F3F series of single-seat carrier fighters, the XF4F-1 was re-planned on the drawing board in the summer of 1936 as a mid-wing monoplane. Though this machine, the XF4F-2, lost out to the Brewster F2A Buffalo, Grumman continued with the XF4F-3 with a more powerful engine and in early 1939 received a French Aéronavale order for 100, the US Navy following with 54 in August. The French aircraft were diverted to Britain and named Martlet I. Production built up with both Twin Wasp and Cyclone engines, folding wings being introduced with the F4F-4, of which Grumman delivered 1,169 plus 220 Martlet IVs for the Fleet Air Arm. Eastern Aircraft Division of General Motors very quickly tooled up and delivered 839 FM-1s and 311 Martlet Vs, the British name then being changed to the US name of Wildcat. Grumman switched to the Avenger, Hellcat and other types, but made F4F-7 reconnaissance versions, weighing 10,328lb and having a 24-hour endurance, as well as a floatplane version. Eastern took over the final mark, the powerful and effective FM-2, delivering 4,777 of this type (including 340 Wildcat VI) in 13 months. A Martlet I shot down a Ju 88 on Christmas Day 1940, and an F4F-3 of VMF-211 destroyed a Japanese bomber at Wake Island on 9 December 1941. Each event was the first of thousands of furious actions from which this quite old fighter emerged with a splendid reputation. Wildcats were especially valuable for their ability to operate from small escort carriers, the pioneer work having been done with British Martlets based in November 1940 on the 5,000 ton captured German vessel *Audacity* on which a flat deck had been built. Noted for their strength and manoeuvrability. Wildcats even sank Japanese submarines and a cruiser.

Above: A 1944 photograph of F4F-4 Wildcats over the Pacific.
By this time the Wildcat was no longer holding the fort by itself.

One of the first F4F-4s to reach the US Navy, this example
is seen with VF-41, the first squadron to be equipped in
November 1941 (when the white star still had a red centre).
Though this Pratt & Whitney-engined version, the first with a
folding wing, was in production only a year, it equipped every
US Navy carrier-based fighter squadron at the start of 1943.

Grumman F6F Hellcat

F6F-1 to -5 Hellcat

Origin: Grumman Aircraft Engineering Corporation.
Type: Single-seat naval fighter; later versions, fighter-bombers and night fighters.
Engine: Early production, one 2,000hp Pratt & Whitney R-2800-10 Double Wasp 18-cylinder two-row radial; from January 1944 (final F6F-3 batch) two-thirds equipped with 2,200hp (water-injection rating) R-2800-10W.
Dimensions: Span 42ft 10in (13·05m); length 33ft 7in (10·2m); height 13ft 1in (3·99m).
Weights: Empty (F6F-3) 9,042lb (4101kg); loaded (F6F-3) 12,186lb (5528kg) clean, 13,228lb (6000kg) maximum, (F6F-5N) 14,250lb (6443kg).
Performance: Maximum speed (F6F-3, -5, clean) 376mph (605km/h); (-5N) 366mph (590km/h); initial climb (typical) 3,240ft (990m)/min; service ceiling (÷3) 37,500ft (11,430m); (-5N) 36,700ft (11,185m); range on internal fuel (typical) 1,090 miles (1755km).
Armament: Standard, six 0·5in Brownings in outer wings with 400 rounds each; a few -5N and -5 Hellcats had two 20mm and four 0·5in. Underwing attachments for six rockets, and centre-section pylons for 2,000lb of bombs.
History: First flight (R-2600) 26 June 1942; (same aircraft, R-2800) 30 July 1942; (production F6F-3) 4 October 1942; production delivery (F6F-3) 16 January 1943; final delivery November 1945.
Users: UK (RN), US (Navy, Marines).

Development: Though pugnacious rather than elegant, the Hellcat was a truly war-winning aircraft. It was designed and developed with great speed, mass-produced at a rate seldom equalled by any other single aircraft factory and used to such good effect that, from the very day of its appearance, ▶

Right: Part of a formation put up by one of the first US Navy squadrons to be equipped with the new F6F-3 (probably VF-8) in early 1943. F4F pilots found conversion relatively painless.

Below right: A Hellcat makes a free takeoff from USS *Enterprise* in 1945. Note the solid phalanx of 40mm and 20mm guns providing devastating firepower all round the ship against Kamikazes.

Below: One of the first F6F-3 Hellcats to have a vertical radio mast, this aircraft was one of those in action at Marcus Island on 31 August 1943, a mere 13 months after the first flight!

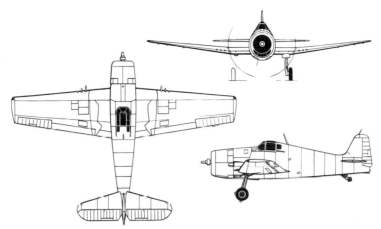

Above: The original F6F-3 variant with F4F-type sloping mast.

Above: One of the first production block of F6F-3 Hellcats. photographed in October 1942 within three months of first flight. It was a pity the F4U could not have rivalled this pace.

Below: This F6F-3, waiting to start engines before an interception mission in 1944, may be the aircraft depicted in the colour profile (with 1942-43 red-bordered markings) at the foot of p. 120.

Above: A fine study of an early F6F-3 about to hit the board deck of a fleet carrier in the Pacific. Note the batsman at right.

Right: An F6F-5 gets a wave-off from an escort carrier and goes round again as the preceding Hellcat disengages from the wire.

the Allies were winning the air war in the Pacific. It began as the XF6F-1, a natural development of the F4F Wildcat with R-2600 Double Cyclone engine. Within a month the more powerful Double Wasp had been substituted and in the autumn of 1942 the production line took shape inside a completely new plant that was less advanced in construction than the Hellcats inside it! This line flowed at an extraordinary rate, helped by the essential rightness of the Hellcat and lack of major engineering changes during subsequent sub-types. Deliveries in the years 1942–45 inclusive were 10, 2,545, 6,139 and 3,578, a total of 12,272 (excluding two prototypes) of which 11,000 were delivered in exactly two years. These swarms of big, beefy fighters absolutely mastered the Japanese, destroying more than 6,000 hostile aircraft (4,947 by USN carrier squadrons, 209 by land-based USMC units and the rest by Allied Hellcat squadrons). The Fleet Air Arm, which originally chose the name Gannet, used Hellcats in Europe as well as throughout the Far East. Unusual features of the F6F were its 334 sq ft of square-tipped wing, with a distinct kink, and backward-retracting landing gear. The F6F-3N and -5N were night fighters with APS-6 radar on a wing pod; the -5K was a drone and the -5P a photographic reconnaissance version. After VJ-day hundreds were sold to many nations.

Grumman F7F Tigercat

F7F-1 to -4N Tigercat

Origin: Grumman Aircraft Engineering Corporation.

Type: Single-seat or two-seat fighter bomber or night fighter (-4N for carrier operation).

Engines: Two Pratt & Whitney R-2800-22W or -34W Double Wasp 18-cylinder two-row radials each rated at 2,100hp (dry) or 2,400hp (water injection).

Dimensions: Span 51ft 6in (15·7m); length (most) 45ft 4in or 45ft 4½in (13·8m); (-3N, -4N) 46ft 10in (14·32m); height (-1, -2) 15ft 2in (4·6m); (-3, -4) 16ft 7in (5·06m).

Weights: Empty (-1) 13,100lb (5943kg); (-3N, -4N) 16,270lb (7379kg); loaded (-1) 22,560lb (10,235kg); (-2N) 26,194lb (11,880kg); (-3) 25,720lb; (-4N) 26,167lb.

Performance: Maximum speed (-1) 427mph (689km/h); (-2N) 421mph; (-3) 435mph; (-4N) 430mph; initial climb (-1) 4,530ft (1380m)/min; service ceiling (-1) 36,200ft; (-2N) 39,800ft (12,131m); (-3) 40,700ft; (-4N) 40,450ft; range on internal fuel (-1) 1,170 miles (1885km); (-2N) 960 miles; (-3) 1,200 miles; (-4N) 810 miles.

Armament: Basic (-1) four 0·5in Browning each with 300 rounds in the nose and four 20mm M-2 cannon each with 200 rounds in the wing roots; outer-wing pylons for six rockets or two 1,000 lb (454kg) bombs; alternatively, one 21in torpedo on fuselage centreline. (-3), nose guns only; (-2N, -3N, -4N) wing guns only.

History: First flight (XF7F-1) December 1943; first service delivery October 1944; final delivery, December 1946.

Users: UK (RN), US (Navy, Marines).

Development: Ordered on the same day as the F6F Hellcat prototypes in June 1941 the F7F was one of the boldest designs in the history of combat aircraft. During the preceding two years the US Navy had keenly studied air war in Europe and noted that the things that appeared to count were the obvious ones; engine power, armament and protective armour and self-

Seen here on factory test over Long Island, the F7F-3 was the final wartime Tigercat variant, with slightly more fuel and engines giving greater power at high altitudes.

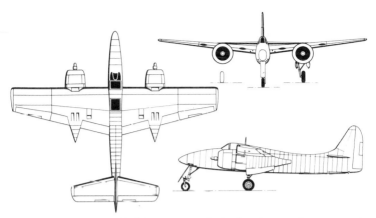

Above: Grumman F7F-3 (post-war -3s had radar or photo noses).

sealing tanks. At a time when the average US Navy fighter had 1,000hp and two machine guns the Bureau of Aeronautics asked Grumman to build a fighter with more than 4,000hp and a weight of fire more than 200 times as great. The company had embarked on a venture along these lines in 1938 with the XF5F, which remained a one-off prototype that was judged not worth the cost and incompatible with Navy carriers. In contrast the F7F was planned on a basis of knowledge and though dramatically heavier and faster than any previous carrier aircraft it was matched with the deck of the large Midway class carriers then under construction. Most, however, were ordered for the Marine Corps for use from land. The F7F-1 of which 34 were built, were single seaters with APS-6 radar in a wing pod. The 66 F7F-2Ns followed, with nose radar in place of guns and the observer in place of the rear fuel tank. The -3 introduced the -34W engine and so had a larger tail; most of the 250 built were -3N night fighters or -3P photographic aircraft. The final models were strengthened -4s, cleared for carrier use, the whole batch being -4Ns. Tigercats arrived at a time when emphasis was rapidly switching to the jet.

Lockheed P-38 Lightning

XP-38 to P-38M, F-4 and F-5, RP and TP conversions

Origin: Lockheed Aircraft Corporation.

Type: Single-seat long-range fighter (see text for variations).

Engines: Two Allison V-1710 vee-12 liquid-cooled; (YP-38) 1,150hp V-1710-27/29 (all P-38 engines handed with opposite propeller rotation, hence pairs of engine sub-type numbers); (P-38E to G) 1,325hp V-1710-49/52 or 51/55; (P-38H and J) 1,425hp V-1710-89/91; (P-38L and M) 1,600hp V-1710-111/113.

Dimensions: Span 52ft (15·86m); length 37ft 10in (11·53m); (F-5G, P-38M and certain "droop-snoot" conversions fractionally longer); height 12ft 10in (3·9m).

Weights: Empty, varied from 11,000lb (4990kg) in YP to average of 12,700lb (5766kg), with heaviest sub-types close to 14,000lb (6350kg); maximum loaded, (YP) 14,348lb (6508kg); (D) 15,500lb; (E) 15,482lb; (F) 18,000lb; (G) 19,800lb; (H) 20,300lb; (L, M) 21,600lb (9798kg).

Performance: Maximum speed (all) 391–414mph (630–666km/h); initial climb (all) about 2,850ft (870m)/min; service ceiling (up to G) 38,000–40,000ft; (H, J, L) 44,000ft (13,410m); range on internal fuel 350–460 miles (563–740km); range at 30,000ft with maximum fuel (late models) 2,260 miles (3650km).

Armament: See "Development" text.

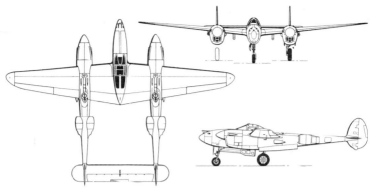

Above: Lockheed P-38J, the mass-produced definitive version.

History: First flight (XP-38) 27 January 1939; (YP-38) 16 September 1940; service delivery (USAAC P-38) 8 June 1941; (F-4) March 1942; (P-38F) September 1942; final delivery September 1945.
Users: France, UK (RAF, briefly), US (AAC/AAF)

Development: In February 1937 the US Army Air Corps issued a specification for a long-range interceptor (pursuit) and escort fighter, calling for a speed of 360mph at 20,000ft and endurance at this speed of one hour. Lockheed, which had never built a purely military design, jumped in with ▶

Left: The first really good and fully combat-ready variant was the P-38F; this P-38F-5 (not to be confused with the F-5 photo variant) served on Guadalcanal with the 347th FG, detached from the 13th Air Force in February 1943.

Below: The F-5E was one of the later series of unarmed photo-reconnaissance Lightnings, based on the P-38J (as here) or the similar L.

both feet and created a revolutionary fighter bristling with innovations and posing considerable technical risks. Powered by two untried Allison engines, with GEC turbochargers recessed into the tops of the tail booms, it had a tricycle landing gear, small central nacelle mounting a 23mm Madsen cannon and four 0·5in Brownings firing parallel directly ahead of the pilot, twin fins, Fowler flaps, cooling radiators on the flanks of the booms and induction intercoolers in the wing leading edges. This box of tricks ran into a ditch on its first taxi test, and two weeks after first flight undershot at Mitchell Field, NY, and was demolished. What made headlines, however, was that it had flown to New York in 7hr 2min, with two refuelling stops, demonstrating a performance which in 1939 seemed beyond belief. The enthusiasm of the Air Corps overcame the doubts and high cost and by 1941 the first YP-38 was being tested, with a 37mm Oldsmobile cannon, two 0·5s and two Colt 0·3s. Thirteen YPs were followed on the Burbank line by 20 P-38s, with one 37mm and four 0·5, plus armour and, in the 36 D models, self-sealing tanks. In March 1940 the British Purchasing Commission had ordered 143 of this type, with the 37mm replaced by a 20mm Hispano and far greater ammunition capacity. The State Department prohibited export of the F2 Allison engine and RAF aircraft, called Lightning I, had early C15 engines without turbochargers, both having right-hand rotation (P-38s had propellers turning outward). The result was poor and the RAF rejected these machines, which were later brought up to US standard. The E model adopted the British name Lightning and the RAF Hispano gun. Within minutes of the US declaration of war, on 7 December 1941, an E shot down an Fw 200C near Iceland, and the P-38 was subsequently in the thick of fighting in North Africa, North West Europe and the Pacific. The F was the first to have inner-wing pylons for 1,000lb bombs, torpedoes, tanks or other stores. By late 1943 new G models were being flown to Europe across the North Atlantic, while in the Pacific 16 aircraft of the 339th Fighter Squadron destroyed Admiral Yamamoto's aircraft 550 miles from their base at Guadalcanal. The J had the intercoolers moved

Above: A fully operational khaki-drab P-38F on test from Burbank in 1942. This was the first variant with drop tanks.

under the engines, changing the appearance, providing room for 55 extra gallons of fuel in the outer wings. Later J models had hydraulically boosted ailerons, but retained the wheel-type lateral control instead of a stick. The L, with higher war emergency power, could carry 4,000lb of bombs or ten rockets, and often formations would bomb under the direction of a lead-ship converted to droop-snoot configuration with a bombardier in the nose. Hundreds were built as F-4 or F-5 photographic aircraft, and the M was a two-seat night fighter with ASH radar pod under the nose. Lightnings towed gliders, operated on skis, acted as fast ambulances (carrying two stretcher cases) and were used for many special ECM missions. Total production was 9,942 and the P-38 made up for slightly inferior manoeuvrability by its range, reliability and multi-role effectiveness.

Below: The "droop-snoot" Lightnings were P-38Js converted in England to carry a bombardier with a Norden precision sight in a glazed nose. They were lead-ships for large formations of Lightnings which released their bombs when they saw the lead do so.

North American NA-73 P-51/A-36 Mustang

P-51 to P-51L, A-36, F-6, Cavalier 750 to 2500, Piper Enforcer and F-82 Twin Mustang

Origin: North American Aviation Inc, Inglewood and Dallas; built under licence by Commonwealth Aircraft Corporation, Australia (and post-war by Cavalier and Piper).

Type: (P-51) single-seat fighter; (A-36) attack bomber; (F-6) reconnaissance; (post-war Cavalier and Piper models) Co-In; (F-82) night fighter.

Engine: (P-51, A, A-36, F-6A) one 1,150hp Allison V-1710-F3R or 1,125hp V-1710-81 vee-12 liquid-cooled; (P-51B, C, D and K, F-6C) one Packard V-1650 (licence-built R-R Merlin 61-series), originally 1,520hp V-1650-3 followed during P-51D run by 1,590hp V-1650-7; (P-51H) 2,218hp V-1650-9; (Cavalier) mainly V-1650-7; (Turbo-Mustang III) 1,740hp Rolls-Royce Dart 510 turboprop; (Enforcer) 2,535hp Lycoming T55-9 turboprop; (F-82F, G, H) two 2,300hp (wet rating) Allison V-1710-143/145.

Dimensions: Span 37ft 0½in (11·29m); (F-82) 51ft 3in (15·61m); length 32ft 2½in (9·81m); (P-51H) 33ft 4in; (F-82E) 39ft 1in (11·88m); height

Below: Merlin-engined P-51B-15, with Malcolm bubble hood in place of the earlier hinged pattern, of the top-scoring outfit the 4th Fighter Group (334th FS) based at Debden, Essex.

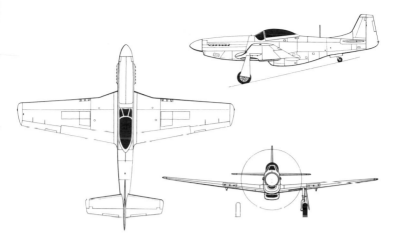

Above: North American P-51D with dorsal fin (P-51K similar).

(P-51, A, A 36, F-6) 12ft 2in (3·72m); (other P-51) 13ft 8in (4·1m); (F-82) 13ft 10in (4·2m).
Weights: Empty (P-51 early V-1710 models, typical) 6,300lb (2858kg); (P-51D) 7,125lb (3230kg); (F-82E) 14,350lb (6509kg); maximum loaded (P-51 early) 8,600lb (3901kg); (P-51D) 11,600lb (5,206kg); (F-82E) 24,864lb (11,276kg).

continued ▶

Below left: An early Merlin-Mustang, from the P-51B-15-NA production block, in olive drab and red-bordered markings in early 1943. These P-51s had only four 0.5in guns.

Below: Most famous of all Mustangs, *Shangri-La* was the personal mount of Capt Don Gentile, top-scorer of the famed 4th FG. His final revised score was 21.8 in the air (more than half gained in the month of March 1944) and 6 in ground strafing. He crashed this aircraft beating up Debden!

Performance: Maximum speed (early P-51) 390mph (628km/h); (P-51D) 437mph (703km/h); (F-82, typical) 465mph (750km/h); initial climb (early) 2,600ft (792m)/min, (P-51D) 3,475ft (1060m)/min; service ceiling (early) 30,000ft (9144m); (P-51D) 41,900ft (12,770m), range with maximum fuel (early) 450 miles (724km); (P-51D) combat range 950 miles, operational range 1,300 miles with drop tanks and absolute range to dry tanks of 2,080 miles; (F-82E) 2,504 miles.

Armament: (RAF Mustang I) four 0·303in in wings, two 0·5in in wings and two 0·5in in lower sides of nose; (Mustang IA and P-51) four 20mm Hispano in wings; (P-51A and B) four 0·5in in wings; (A-36A) six 0·5in in wings and wing racks for two 500lb (227kg) bombs; (all subsequent P-51 production models) six 0·5in Browning MG53-2 with 270 or 400 rounds each, and wing racks for tanks or two 1,000lb (454kg) bombs; (F-82, typical) six 0·5in in centre wing, six or eight pylons for tanks, radars or up to 4,000lb weapons.

History: First flight (NA-73X) 26 October 1940; (production RAF Mustang I) 1 May 1941; service delivery (RAF) October 1941; first flight

Above: As Inglewood and Dallas poured out the war-winning P-51D, so did Allied airpower swell in every theatre. These served with the 8th AF's 361st FG, in early 1944 based at Bottisham but later at St Dizier, France (ship 2106811 is a P-51B).

(Merlin conversion) 13 October 1942; (P-51B) December 1942; final delivery (P-51H) November 1945; first flight (XP-82A) 15 April 1945; final delivery (F-82G) April 1949.

Users: (Wartime) Australia, Canada, China (and AVG), Netherlands, New Zealand, Poland, South Africa, Soviet Union, Sweden, UK (RAF), USA (AAC/AAF).

Development: In April 1940 the British Air Purchasing Commission concluded with "Dutch" Kindelberger, chairman of North American Aviation, an agreement for the design and development of a completely new fighter for the RAF. Designed, built and flown in 117 days, this silver prototype was the start of the most successful fighter programme in history. ▶

The RAF received 620 Mustang I, 150 IA and 50 II, while the US Army adopted the type with 500 A-36A and 310 P-51A. In 1942 the brilliant airframe was matched with the Merlin engine, yielding the superb P-51B, bulged-hood C (Mustang III) and teardrop-canopy D (Mustang IV), later C and all D models having six 0·5in guns and a dorsal fin. The final models were the K (different propeller) and better-shaped, lighter H, the fastest of all at 487mph. Total production was 15,586. Mustang and P-51 variants served mainly in Europe, their prime mission being the almost incredible one of flying all the way from British bases to targets of the 8th AF deep in Germany – Berlin or beyond – escorting heavies and gradually establishing Allied air superiority over the heart of Germany. After the war the Mustang proved popular with at least 55 nations, while in 1947–49 the US Air Force bought 272 examples of the appreciably longer Twin Mustang (two Allison-powered fuselages on a common wing), most of them radar night fighters which served in Korea. In 1945–48 Commonwealth Aircraft of Australia made under licence 200 Mustangs of four versions. In 1967 the P-51 was put back into production by Cavalier for the US Air Force and other customers, and the turboprop Turbo III and Enforcer versions were developed for the Pave Coin programme for Forward Air Control and light attack missions. Many of the new or remanufactured models of 1968–75 are two-seaters.

Right: Until late 1943 the only variants in service had the Allison engine; this example is a cannon-armed P-51 (NA-91).

Below: Deadly sight for a Jap was this swarm of P-51Ds of the 45th FS, 15th FG, 7th Fighter Command, 20th AF, on Iwo Jima.

Above: Return of a P-51D of the 353rd Fighter Group, 8th AF, to Raydon, Suffolk.

Left: The Mustang III, with bulged Malcolm hood, of S/L Horbaczewski, CO of 315 Sqn at Brenzett. He once rescued a fellow-Pole from capture and flew back with him in the Mustang cockpit!

Northrop P-61 Black Widow
P-61A, B and C and F-15 (RF-61C) Reporter

Origin: Northrop Aircraft Inc, Hawthorne, California.
Type: (P-61) three-seat night fighter; (F-15) two-seat strategic reconnaissance.
Engines: Two Pratt & Whitney R-2800 Double Wasp 18-cylinder two-row radials; (P-61A) 2,000hp R-2800-10; (B) 2,000hp R-2800-65; (C and F-15) 2,800hp (wet rating) R-2800-73.
Dimensions: Span 66ft (20·12m); length (A) 48ft 11in (14·92m); (B, C) 49ft 7in (15·1m); (F-15) 50ft 3in (15·3m); height (typical) 14ft 8in (4·49m).
Weights: Empty (typical P-61) 24,000lb (10,886kg); (F-15) 22,000lb (9979kg); maximum loaded (A) 32,400lb (14,696kg); (B) 38,000lb (17,237kg); (C) 40,300lb (18,280kg); (F-15, clean) 28,000lb (12,700kg).
Performance: maximum speed (A, B) 366mph (590km/h); (C) 430mph (692km/h); (F-15) 440mph (708km/h); initial climb (A, B) 2,200ft (670m)/min; (C, F-15) 3,000ft (914m)/min; service ceiling (A, B) 33,000ft (10,060m); (C, F-15) 41,000ft (12,500m); range with maximum fuel (A) 500 miles; (B, C) 2,800 miles (4500km); (F.15) 4,000 miles (6440km).
Armament: Four Fixed 20mm M-2 cannon in belly, firing ahead (plus, in first 37 A, last 250 B and all C) electric dorsal turret with four 0·5in remotely controlled from front or rear sight station and fired by pilot; (B and C) underwing racks for 6,400lb load; (F-15A) no armament.
History: First flight (XP-61) 21 May 1942; service delivery (A) May 1944; first flight (F-15A) 1946.
User: USA (AAF).

Development: The first aircraft ever ordered to be designed explicitly as a night fighter, the XP-61 prototypes were ordered in January 1941 on the basis of combat reports from the early radar-equipped fighters of the RAF. A very big aircraft, the P-61 had the new SCR-720 AI radar in the nose, the armament being mounted well back above and below the rather lumpy nacelle housing pilot, radar operator and gunner with front and rear sighting stations. The broad wing had almost full-span double-slotted flaps, very small ailerons and lateral-control spoilers in an arrangement years ahead of its time. Black-painted (hence the name), the P-61A entered service with the 18th Fighter Group in the South Pacifice and soon gained successes there and in Europe. Buffet from the turret led to this soon being deleted, but the B and C had pylons for the very heavy load of four 250 gal tanks or 6,400lb (2900kg) bombs. Total production was 941, followed by 35 slim photo-reconnaissance versions.

continued ▶

Below: Though late in reaching the war, the P-61 proved a tough and capable aircraft. This P-61A-5 was assigned in July 1944 to the 9th AF's 422nd NFS, based at Scorton, in North Yorkshire.

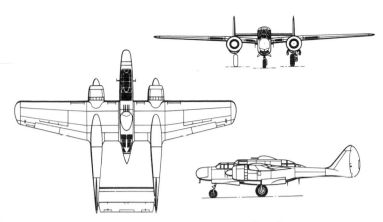

Above: Northrop P-61A with dorsal turret fitted.

Above: Despite its great size the P-61 had very good manoeuvrability, in part because of the patented spoiler-type lateral control and Deceleron aileron/airbrake surfaces. Most of the P-61s that reached Europe were engaged in night ground-attack missions; the P-61B and C could carry no less than 6,400lb of bombs.

Above: Most of the early production P-61As went to the 422nd NFS. This is 42-5578 pictured over West Germany late in the war. At this time the squadron had moved to Etain, in France.

Below: Another of the early P-61As of the 422nd, pictured at its dispersal at Scorton in the autumn of 1944, just before moving to France. The rival 425th NFS was then operating at Charmy Down.

Republic P-47 Thunderbolt
P-47B, C, D, M and N

Origin: Republic Aviation Corporation.
Type: Single-seat fighter; (D and N) fighter-bomber.
Engine: One Pratt & Whitney R-2800 Double Wasp 18-cylinder two-row radial; (B) 2,000hp R-2800-21; (C, most D) 2,300hp R-2800-59; (M, N) 2,800hp R-2800-57 or -77 (emergency wet rating).
Dimensions: Span 40ft 9¼in (12·4m); length (B) 34ft 10in; (C, D, M, N) 36ft 1¼in (11·03m); height (B) 12ft 8in; (C, D) 14ft 2in (4·3m); (M, N) 14ft 8in.
Weights: Empty (B) 9,010lb (4087kg); (D) 10,700lb (4853kg); maximum loaded (B) 12,700lb (5760kg); (C) 14,925lb; (D) 19,400lb (8800kg); (M) 14,700lb; (N) 21,200lb (9616kg).
Performance: Maximum speed (B) 412mph; (C) 433mph; (D) 428mph (690km/h); (M) 470mph; (N) 467mph (751km/h); initial climb (typical) 2,800ft (855m)/min; service ceiling (B) 38,000ft; (C-N) 42,000–43,000ft (13,000m); range on internal fuel (B) 575 miles; (D) 1,000 miles (1600km); ultimate range (drop tanks) (D) 1,900 miles (3060km); (N) 2,350 miles (3800km).
Armament: (Except M) eight 0·5in Colt-Browning M-2 in wings, each with 267, 350 or 425 rounds (M) six 0·5in; (D and N) three to five racks for external load of tanks, bombs or rockets to maximum of 2,500lb (1134kg).

Below: This colourful
P-47D-25 belonged to the
352nd FS, 353rd FG, Raydon.

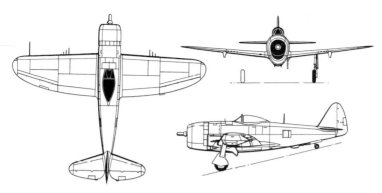

Above: Republic P-47D-25 prior to addition of dorsal fin.

History: First flight (XP-47B) 6 May 1941; production delivery (B) 18 March 1942; final delivery (N) September 1945.
Users: Australia, Brazil, France, Soviet Union, UK (RAF), USA (AAF).

Development: Before the United States entered World War II it was eagerly digesting the results of air combats in Europe and, in 1940, existing plans by Republic's chief designer Alexander Kartveli were urgently replaced by sketches for a much bigger fighter with the new R-2800 engine. ▶

Below: Despite their yellow engine cowls – later to denote the 361st Fighter Group of the 8th Air Force – these two early P-47Cs were photographed over Long Island in 1942 before any of this type were assigned to the 361st. Curiously, like the Typhoon the P-47 was thought to be readily mistaken for the Fw 190, and most early examples in the European theatre had white bands over the tail surfaces and white engine cowls to avoid confusion. Early models, prior to the bubble canopy, were called "razorbacks".

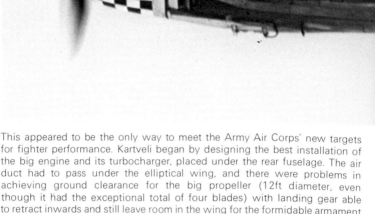

This appeared to be the only way to meet the Army Air Corps' new targets for fighter performance. Kartveli began by designing the best installation of the big engine and its turbocharger, placed under the rear fuselage. The air duct had to pass under the elliptical wing, and there were problems in achieving ground clearance for the big propeller (12ft diameter, even though it had the exceptional total of four blades) with landing gear able to retract inwards and still leave room in the wing for the formidable armament of eight 0·5in guns. After severe and protracted technical difficulties the P-47B was cleared for production in early 1942 and at the beginning of 1943 two fighter groups equipped with the giant new fighter (one the famed 56th, to become top scorers in Europe) joined the 8th AF in Britain to begin escorting B-17 and B-24 heavies. Their value was dramatically increased when they began to carry drop tanks and fly all the way to the target. The same capability turned the big and formidable fighter into a much-feared bomber and, with devastating firepower, vast numbers of P-47Ds strafed and bombed throughout the European and Pacific theatres until the end of World War II. Republic's output of D models (12,602) is the largest

Above: An early "razorback" P-47D, in D-Day markings and the checkered nose of the 78th FG based at Duxford.

total of one sub-type of any fighter in history, total production of the "Jug" amounting to 15,660. The lightweight M was too late for its role of chasing flying bombs but scored successes against the Me 262 and Ar 234 jets, while the long-range P-47N matched the M fuselage with a bigger wing for the Pacific war. There were numerous experimental versions, one of which reached 504mph. After World War II the "Jug" was popular with many air forces until well into the 1950s.

Below left: The name *Chunky* was particularly apt for this bombed and tanked P-47D-10; the popular name "Jug" was derived from Juggernaut.

Below: The P-47N's long-span wing with zero-length rocket launchers and extra fuel raised internal capacity to 594Imp gallons.

Vought V-166B F4U Corsair

F4U-1 to -7, F3A, FG, F2G and AU

Origin: Chance Vought Division of United Aircraft Corporation; also built by Brewster and Goodyear.

Type: Single-seat carrier-based fighter-bomber (sub-variants, see text).

Engine: (F4U-1) 2,000hp Pratt & Whitney R-2800-8(B) Double Wasp 18-cylinder two-row radial; (-1A) 2,250hp R-2800-8(W) with water injection; (-4) 2,450hp R-2800-18W with water-methanol; (-5) 2,850hp R-2800-32(E) with water-methanol; (F2G) 3,000hp P&W R-4360 Wasp Major 28-cylinder four-row radial.

Dimensions: Span 40ft 11¾in (12·48m), (British, 39ft 7in); length 33ft 8¼in (10·27m); (-1, -3) 33ft 4in; (-5N and -7) 34ft 6in; height 14ft 9¼in (4·49m); (-1, -2) 16ft 1in.

Weights: Empty (-1A) 8,873lb (4025kg); (-5, typical) 9,900lb (4490kg); maximum loaded (-1A) 14,000lb (6350kg); (-5) 15,079lb (6840kg); (AU-1) 19,398lb.

Performance: Maximum speed (-1A) 395mph (635km/h); (-5) 462mph (744km/h); initial climb (-1A) 2,890ft (880m)/min; (-5) 4,800ft (1463m)/min; service ceiling (-1A) 37,000ft (11,280m); (-5) 44,000ft (13,400m); range on internal fuel, typically 1,000 miles (1609km).

Armament: See "Development" text.

History: First flight (XF4U) 29 May 1940; (production -1) June 1942; combat delivery July 1942; final delivery (-7) December 1952.

Users: (Wartime) Mexico, New Zealand, UK (RN), USA (Navy, Marines).

Development: Designed by Rex Beisel and Igor Sikorsky, the inverted-gull-wing Corsair was one of the greatest combat aircraft in history. Planned to use the most powerful engine and biggest propeller ever fitted to a fighter, the prototype was the first US warplane to exceed 400mph and outperformed all other American aircraft. Originally fitted with two fuselage and two wing guns, it was replanned with six 0·5in Browning MG 53-2 in the folding outer wings, each with about 390 rounds. Action with land-based Marine squadrons began in the Solomons in February 1943; from then on the Corsair swiftly gained air supremacy over the previously untroubled Japanese. The -1C had four 20mm cannon, and the -1D and most subsequent types carried a 160gal drop tank and two 1,000lb (907kg) ▶

Below: This F4U-1D was typical of the late-war production by Chance Vought and Goodyear. It is shown with rockets but no tanks in Marines livery.

Right: This F4U-1A, with hook removed for land-based operation, was one of 424 supplied in the final year of the war to the RNZAF. No 5315 was assigned to 18 Sqn, based at Bougainville from January 1945, and saw intensive combat duties throughout the Solomons and Guadalcanal.

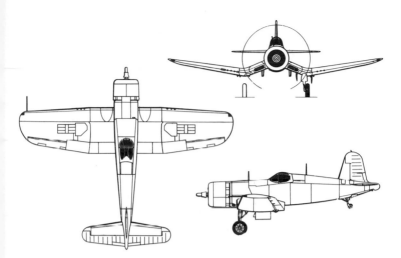

Above: F4U-1D with normal wingtip and armament.

Above: Taken in the spring of 1945, this photograph shows a Corsair (probably an F4U-1A) of the Marine Corps (probably VMF-124) making a carrier landing. A few units, such as VF-17 and VMF-214, gained widespread publicity, but the majority were seldom visited by official reporters.

bombs or eight rockets. Many hundreds of P versions carried cameras, and N variants had an APS-4 or -6 radar in a wing pod for night interceptions. Brewster made 735 F3A, and Goodyear 4,008 FG versions, but only ten of the fearsome F2G. Fabric-skinned wings became metal in the post-war -5, most of which had cannon, while the 110 AU-1 attack bombers carried a 4,000lb load in Korea at speeds seldom exceeding 240mph! In December 1952 the last of 12,571 Corsairs came off the line after a longer production run (in terms of time) than any US fighter prior to the Phantom.

Above: An apparently new F4U-1, with revised canopy, flying in British waters in 1943. It bears no unit markings but is probably in Marine Corps hands, with the 1943 paint scheme of gloss/non-specular sea blue, intermediate blue and white

Below: Running up on the Vought ramp at Stratford, JT531 was a Corsair II (F4U-1D) of the Fleet Air Arm. First model to operate from carriers, the Corsair II had clipped wings to fit below decks.

OTHER NATIONS

Of course, many important countries such as Argentina, Sweden and Switzerland did not officially participate in World War II and their aircraft are absent from this book. Other countries, such as Poland and the Netherlands, were overrun within weeks or days by the Nazi armies, and few of their aircraft survived to play any ongoing role. Australia, however, was a special case.

Geographically well separated from potential enemies, the Commonwealth of Australia had spent only token amounts on defence and had virtually no capability for manufacturing warplanes until after the start of World War II. But, partly through the initiative of Wing Commander Lawrence Wackett, who had formed Tugan Aircraft and then, in 1936, registered Commonwealth Aircraft Corporation, the germ of a planemaking industry did exist. This was strengthened by the decision in January 1939 to build the British Beaufort under Bristol licence, powered by locally made Twin Wasp engines.

These engines were the only ones available when, in January 1942, Australia found itself facing invasion by the all-conquering Japanese. Within weeks Wackett had completed the basic design of a tough but inevitably second-rate fighter, the Boomerang, to use the Twin Wasp. Like most things Australian, it had no frills but worked. To the end of the war Boomerangs were to be found "looking into the whites of the enemy's eyes",

This American-engined Dutch Fokker G.I was intended for Spain but was commandeered for home defence at the Fokker works. It flew a single mission on 13 May 1940.

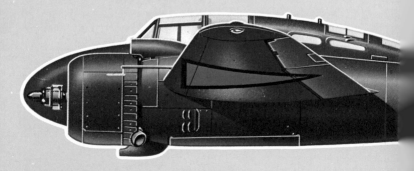

typically serving as a target marker for strikes by Hellcats, Corsairs or even large bombers.

In 1919 in Amsterdam Anthony Fokker got started as a planemaker by illegally tricking his former enemies, the Allies, into letting through trainloads of aircraft materials and parts. He became the most successful constructor in Western Europe, with both military and civil types. The D.XXI fighter was an effective intermediate design with an unbraced monoplane wing and variable-pitch propeller but old-fashioned structure and fixed landing gear. The small force was soon eliminated by the Luftwaffe. The big all-metal G.I created an international sensation when the prototype appeared at the Paris airshow in 1936; its firepower was exceptional, and matched by general size and power. On 10 May 1940, however, there were simply too few to make any difference.

Poland presented an even sorrier picture. In the mid-1930s its air force had been one of the strongest and best trained in Europe, and the large force of fighter regiments equipped with the P.11 would have deterred any aggressor. By 1939, however, they were out of date. There was, it is true, a successor, the PZL P.50 Jastrzab. Only one prototype was flying when the Germans invaded, and that was shot down by Polish AA gunners who thought it must be German.

Commonwealth Boomerang

CA-12 to CA-19 Boomerang
(data for CA-12)

Origin: Commonwealth Aircraft Corporation, Australia.
Type: Single-seat fighter.
Engine: 1,200hp Pratt & Whitney R-1830-S3C4G Twin Wasp 14-cylinder two-row radial.
Dimensions: Span 36ft 3in (11m); length 25ft 6in (7·77m); height 11ft 6in (3·5m).
Weights: Empty 5,450lb (2474kg); loaded 7,600lb (3450kg).
Performance: Maximum speed 296mph (474km/h); service ceiling 29,000ft (8845m); range at 190mph (304km/h) 930 miles (1490km).
Armament: Normally, two 20mm Hispano cannon and four 0·303in Browning machine guns in wings.
History: First flight 29 May 1942; first delivery August 1942; final deliveries, early 1944.
User: Australia.

Development: When Australia suddenly found itself in the front line, in December 1941, it had no modern fighters save a few Buffaloes supplied to the RAF in Singapore. To try to produce a stop-gap quickly the Commonwealth Aircraft Corporation at Fishermen's Bend, Melbourne, decided to design and build their own. But the design team, under Wing Commander Laurence J. Wackett, was severely restricted. The new fighter had to be based on the familiar North American trainer series, which since 1938 had served as the basis for the excellent Wirraway general-purpose combat machine and trainer, of which 755 were made by CAC by 1946. Moreover the only powerful engine available was the 1,200hp Twin Wasp, judged by 1942 to be much too low-powered for first-line fighters elsewhere. Despite these restrictions the resulting machine was tough, outstandingly manoeuvrable and by no means outclassed by the Japanese opposition. Wackett's team worked day and night to design the CA-12 in a matter of weeks and build and fly the prototype in a further 14 weeks. Testing and production went ahead together and, as there were no real snags, the first of 105 CA-12s were soon fighting in New Guinea. There followed 95 CA-13s with minor changes and 49 CA-19s, as well as a CA-14 with turbocharged engine and square tail. Boomerangs did not carry bombs but often marked targets for "heavies" and undertook close support with their guns.

Above right: Part of a formation of Boomerangs of No 5 Sqn, RAAF, operating from Bougainville, New Guinea, in 1944.

Below right: The second production CA-12, at roll-out.

Below: This Boomerang, actually the aircraft nearest the camera in the photograph above right, is a CA-13 incorporating numerous minor changes as the result of combat experience.

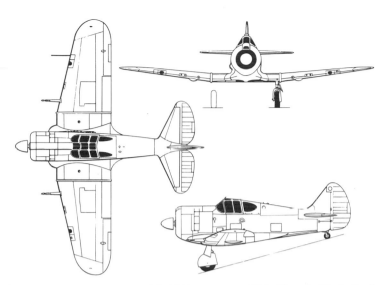

Above: Commonwealth CA-13 Boomerang (CA-12 and -19 similar).

Fokker D.XXI

D.XXI (D.21)

Origin: NV Fokker, Netherlands; licence-built by Valtion Lentokonetehdas, Finland; Haerens Flyvertroppernes Vaerkstader, Denmark; Spanish Republican Government plant.

Type: Single-seat fighter.

Engine: (Dutch) one 830hp Bristol Mercury VIII nine-cylinder radial; (Danish) 645hp Mercury VIS; (Finnish) 825hp Pratt & Whitney R-1535-SB4-G Twin Wasp Junior 14-cylinder two-row radial.

Dimensions: Span 36ft 1in (11m); length (Mercury) 26ft 11in (8·22m); (R-1535) 26ft 3in (8m); height 9ft 8in (2·94m).

Weights: Empty (Mercury) 3,180lb (1442kg); (R-1535) 3,380lb (1534kg); loaded (Mercury) 4,519lb (2050kg); (R-1535) 4,820lb (2186kg).

Performance: Maximum speed (Mercury VIII) 286mph (480km/h); (R-1535) 272mph (439km/h); climb to 9,842ft (3000m) 3·5min (Mercury); 4·5min (R-1535); service ceiling (Mercury) 36,090ft (11,000m); (R-1535) 32,000ft (9750m); range (Mercury) 590 miles (950km); (R-1353) 559 miles (900km).

Armament: (Dutch) four 7·9mm FN-Brownings, two in fuselage and two in wings; (Danish) two Madsen 7·9mm in wings and two Madsen 20mm cannon in underwing blisters; (Finnish) four 7·7mm machine guns in outer wings.

History: First flight, 27 March 1936; service delivery (Dutch) January 1938, (Finnish production) June 1938, (Danish production) 1939.

Users: Denmark, Finland, Netherlands.

Development: In the second half of the 1930s any sound warplane that was generally available could be sure of attracting widespread interest. The Fokker D.XXI came from a company with a great reputation all over the world, and though it was designed – by Ir. E. Schatzki, in 1935 – purely to meet the requirements of the Netherlands East Indies Army Air Service, it became the leading fighter of three major European nations and was planned as a standard type by a fourth. This was as well for Fokker, because the plans of the original customer were changed and a contract was never signed. Yet the little fighter was all one would expect: neat, tough and highly manoeuvrable, with good performance and heavy armament. It marked the transition between the fabric-covered biplane and the stressed-skin monoplane. The wing was wood, with bakelite/ply skin. The fuselage was welded steel tube, with detachable metal panels back to the cockpit and fabric on

Below: 26th of the 36 D.XXI fighters bought for the home LVA, assigned to the 2e Jachtvliegtuigafdeling at Amsterdam Schipol. Orange "neutrality" markings were adopted in October 1939.

Right: Shown in the pre-war Dutch national markings, the second and fourth D.XXI fighters escort the new Fokker T.V. (T.5) twin-Pegasus bomber.

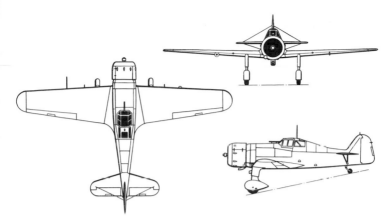

Above: Fokker D.XXI of original Dutch (Mercury engine) type.

the rear fuselage and tail. Landing gear was fixed. The prototype flew at Welschap on a Mercury VIS engine, and in May 1937 the home government ordered 36 with a more powerful Mercury, supplied from Bristol. There were many Fokker projects for developed D.XXIs with retractable landing gear and other engines, but the production aircraft was generally similar to the prototype. In the seventh (No 217) test pilot H. Leegstra set a Dutch height record at 37,250ft. Meanwhile production of a modified version was getting under way for Finland, which bought seven with a manufacturing licence. Denmark followed with an order for three and a manufacturing licence, and the fourth to adopt the D.XXI was Republican Spain. The latter set up a new plant and was about to start accepting deliveries when the area was overrun by Nationalist forces. The VL (Finnish state factory) delivered 38 in 1938–39 and all of them participated very successfully in air battles against the Soviet forces from the start of the Soviet invasion on 30 November 1939. The D.XXI was put into accelerated production, but as all the Finnish-built Mercuries were needed for Blenheims the Finnish D.XXI was redesigned to take the heavier but less powerful Twin Wasp Junior, 55 of this type being built (one having retractable landing gear). The Danish Royal Army Aircraft Factory gradually delivered ten with low-rated Mercury and two cannon, eight being taken over during the German invasion in March 1940. Finally, on 10 May 1940 the 29 combat-ready aircraft in Holland fought round the clock until their ammunition ran out on the third day.

Fokker G.I
G.Ia and G.Ib

Origin: NV Fokker, Netherlands.

Type: Three-seat (G.Ib, two-seat) heavy fighter and close-support.

Engines: (G.Ia) two 830hp Bristol Mercury VIII nine-cylinder radials; (G.Ib) two 750hp Pratt & Whitney R-1535-SB4-G Twin Wasp Junior 14-cylinder radials.

Dimensions: Span (G.Ia) 56ft 3¼in (17·2m); (G.Ib) 54ft 1½in (16·5m); length, (G.Ia) 37ft 8⅔in (11·5m); (G.Ib) 33ft 9½in (10·3m); height 11ft 1¾in (3·4m).

Weights: Empty (G.Ia) 7,326lb (3323kg); (G.Ib) 6,930lb (3143kg); loaded, (G.Ia) 10,560lb (4790kg); (G.Ib) 10,520lb (4772kg).

Performance: Maximum speed (G.Ia) 295mph (475km/h); (G.Ib) 268mph (430km/h); time to climb to 19,680ft (6000m), (G.Ia) 8·9min; (G.Ib) 12·1min; service ceiling, (G.Ia) 30,500ft (9300m); (G.Ib) 28,535ft (8695m); range, (G.Ia) 945 miles (1520km); (G.Ib) 913 miles (1469km).

Armament: (G.Ia) row of eight 7·9mm FN-Browning machine guns fixed in nose, one similar gun manually aimed in tailcone; internal bomb bay for load of 880lb (400kg). (G.Ib) two 23mm Madsen cannon and two 7·9mm FN-Brownings in nose, otherwise same.

History: First flight, 16 March 1937; service delivery, May 1938.

Users: Denmark, Netherlands, Sweden.

Development: Appearance of the prototype G.I at the 1936 Paris Salon caused a sensation. The concept of a large twin-engined fighter was novel, and the devastating armament of the G.I caused it to be called "Le Faucheur" (the Grim Reaper). Nations practically queued to test-fly the Hispano-

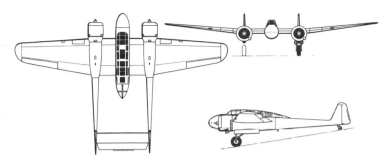

Above: Fokker G.I of original (Mercury engine G.Ia) type.

engined prototype and the first sale was 12 to Republican Spain in June 1937. Meanwhile the home LVA eventually signed for 36 of a much altered version with a third crew-member (radio operator) and Mercury engines in a larger airframe. Finland sought a licence, Sweden bought 18 and Denmark bought nine plus a licence. The Dutch placed an embargo on export of the Spanish aircraft, called G.Ib, and when Germany swept into Holland on 10 May 1940 these were still lined up at Schiphol. Guns were hastily taken from crashed or damaged aircraft and fitted to the Spanish machines which were thrown into the fight. The 23 combat-ready G.Ia fighters likewise fought until all were destroyed save one (in which, in 1942, two senior Fokker pilots escaped to England). There were several non-standard G.Is, including one with a ventral observation cupola. All surviving or unfinished aircraft were impressed into the Luftwaffe and used as combat trainers and tugs.

Left: This Twin Wasp Junior G.I (so-called "G.Ib") was one of those confiscated by the Dutch and parked at Schiphol on 10 May 1940. Hurriedly painted in LVA markings and number 346, it was assigned to 4 JaVA but on 13 May had brake failure and was captured intact by the Luftwaffe.

Below: The first production G.Ia (Mercuries) seen in May 1938.

PZL P.11

P.11a, 11b and 11c

Origin: Państwowe Zakłady Lotnicze, Poland.
Type: Single-seat fighter.
Engine: One Bristol-designed nine-cylinder radial; (11a) 500hp Skoda Mercury IVS2; (11b) 595hp IAR Gnome-Rhône K9 (Jupiter); (11c) 645hp PZL Mercury VIS2.
Dimensions: Span 35ft 2in (10·72m); length 24ft 9in or 24ft 9½in (7·55m); height 9ft 4in (2·85m).
Weights: Empty (11c) 2,524lb (1145kg); loaded 3,960lb (1795kg).
Performance: Maximum speed (11c) 242mph (390km/h); initial climb 2,625ft (800m)/min; service ceiling 36,090ft (11,000m); range (economic cruise, no combat) 503 miles (810km).
Armament: (11a) two 7·7mm (0·303in) Browning, each with 700 rounds, in sides of fuselage; (11c) two 7·7mm KM Wz 33 machine guns, each with 500 rounds, in sides of fuselage, and two more, each with 300 rounds, inside wing at junction of struts; provision for two 27lb (12·25kg) bombs.
History: First flight (P.11/I) August 1931; (production P.11a) June 1933.
Users: Bulgaria (P.24), Greece (P.24), Poland (P.11c), Romania (P.11b, P.24).

Development: Having hired brilliant young designer Zygmund Pulaski at its formation in 1928, the Polish PZL (National Aero Factory) set itself to building gull-winged monoplane fighters of outstanding quality. All the early production models were powered by Polish-built Jupiter engines, and large numbers of P.7a fighters formed the backbone of the young Polish Air Force. The P.11 was the natural successor, but when the prototype was about to fly Pulaski was killed in a crash and his place was taken by W. Jakimiuk (later designer for D. H. Canada and SNCASE). The first P.11 was powered by a Gnome-Rhône Jupiter and subsequent prototypes by a Mistral and Mercury from the same source, but after prolonged trials the P.11a went into production with the Polish-built Mercury IVS. In 1934 the fuselage was redesigned to improve pilot view by lowering the engine and raising the pilot (11c). A new tail and modified wings were introduced and provision was made for two wing guns and radio, but these were usually not available for fitting. The final production model was the export version of the 11a, the 11b, which was built in Romania as the IAR P.11f. Many

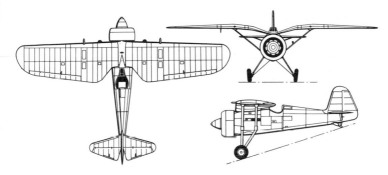

Above: PZL P.11c (showing two extra guns in the wings).

further developments were planned, but the main fighter force defending Poland in September 1939 comprised 12 squadrons of P.11c, most with only two guns and operating with no warning system in chaotic conditions. They nevertheless destroyed 126 Luftwaffe aircraft for the loss of 114 of their own number. Final PZL fighter was the P.24 family, of which there were many variants produced entirely for export. Most had a 970hp Gnome-Rhône 14N engine, and two cannon and two machine guns.

Above: P.11c fighters of the Dyon III/3, 3rd Air Regiment, pictured during the aviation parade at Warsaw in August 1936, when the Polish Army Air Force was one of the strongest and most modern in Europe. In the fighting of September 1939 Dyon III/3 distinguished itself as the highest-scoring of all the Polish fighter units.

Left: A PZL P.11c depicted in new condition and with the full planned armament of four KM Wz 33 machine guns, as fitted to only about one-third of the 175 aircraft of this type delivered for Polish use. Another fault was failure to procure radio sets for all but a small number of the fighters, though it had been intended that all should be so equipped. The P.11c was popularly called Jedenastka (the eleventh); this particular example served with 113 Sqn, 3rd Air Regiment.

GUIDES IN THIS SERIES...........

AN ILLUSTRATED GUIDE TO
ALLIED FIGHTERS OF WORLD WAR II
160 fact-packed pages in colour
Descriptions of over 40 aircraft types, plus many variants
Over 110 photographs, many in colour
More than 120 detailed line drawings
Over 60 colour drawings
Bill Gunston

AN ILLUSTRATED GUIDE TO
WORLD WAR II TANKS AND FIGHTING VEHICLES
39 formidable tanks and many variants described in 160 fact-packed pages in colour
More than 170 superb illustrations, including action photographs and highly detailed colour drawings
Edited by Christopher F. Foss

AN ILLUSTRATED GUIDE TO
RIFLES AND SUB-MACHINE GUNS
45 modern rifles and 35 sub-machine guns All photographed in full colour 35,000 words of text
Major Frederick Myatt M.C.

AN ILLUSTRATED GUIDE TO
GERMAN, ITALIAN AND JAPANESE FIGHTERS OF WORLD WAR II
Major Fighters and Attack Aircraft of the Axis Powers
160 fact-packed pages in colour
Descriptions of well over 90 aircraft types, plus many variants
120 dramatic photographs, many in colour
More than 180 detailed line drawings
Over 50 colour drawings
Bill Gunston

AN ILLUSTRATED GUIDE TO
BOMBERS OF WORLD WAR II
160 fact-packed pages in colour
Descriptions of well over 50 aircraft types, plus many variants
More than 140 detailed line drawings
90 dramatic photographs, many in colour
Over 40 colour drawings
Bill Gunston

AN ILLUSTRATED GUIDE TO
MODERN FIGHTERS AND ATTACK AIRCRAFT
Fact-packed descriptions of 60 of the world's most exciting warplanes
120 action photographs 180 line drawings 34 superb colour profiles
Bill Gunston

AN ILLUSTRATED GUIDE TO
MODERN TANKS AND FIGHTING VEHICLES
The world's major combat vehicles described in 160 fact-packed pages
120 action photographs, most in colour Superbly detailed technical drawings
Edited by Ray Bonds

AN ILLUSTRATED GUIDE TO
MODERN WARSHIPS
Over 60 of the world's most exciting warships
160 fact-packed pages in colour
130 action photographs Over 60 technical drawings
Hugh Lyon

✷ Each has 160 fact-filled pages
✷ Each is colourfully illustrated with more than one hundred dramatic photographs, and often with superb technical drawings
✷ Each contains concisely presented data and accurate descriptions of major international weapons
✷ Each represents tremendous value

Further titles in this series are in preparation
Your military library will be incomplete without them

PRINTED IN BELGIUM BY

proost
INTERNATIONAL BOOK PRODUCTION